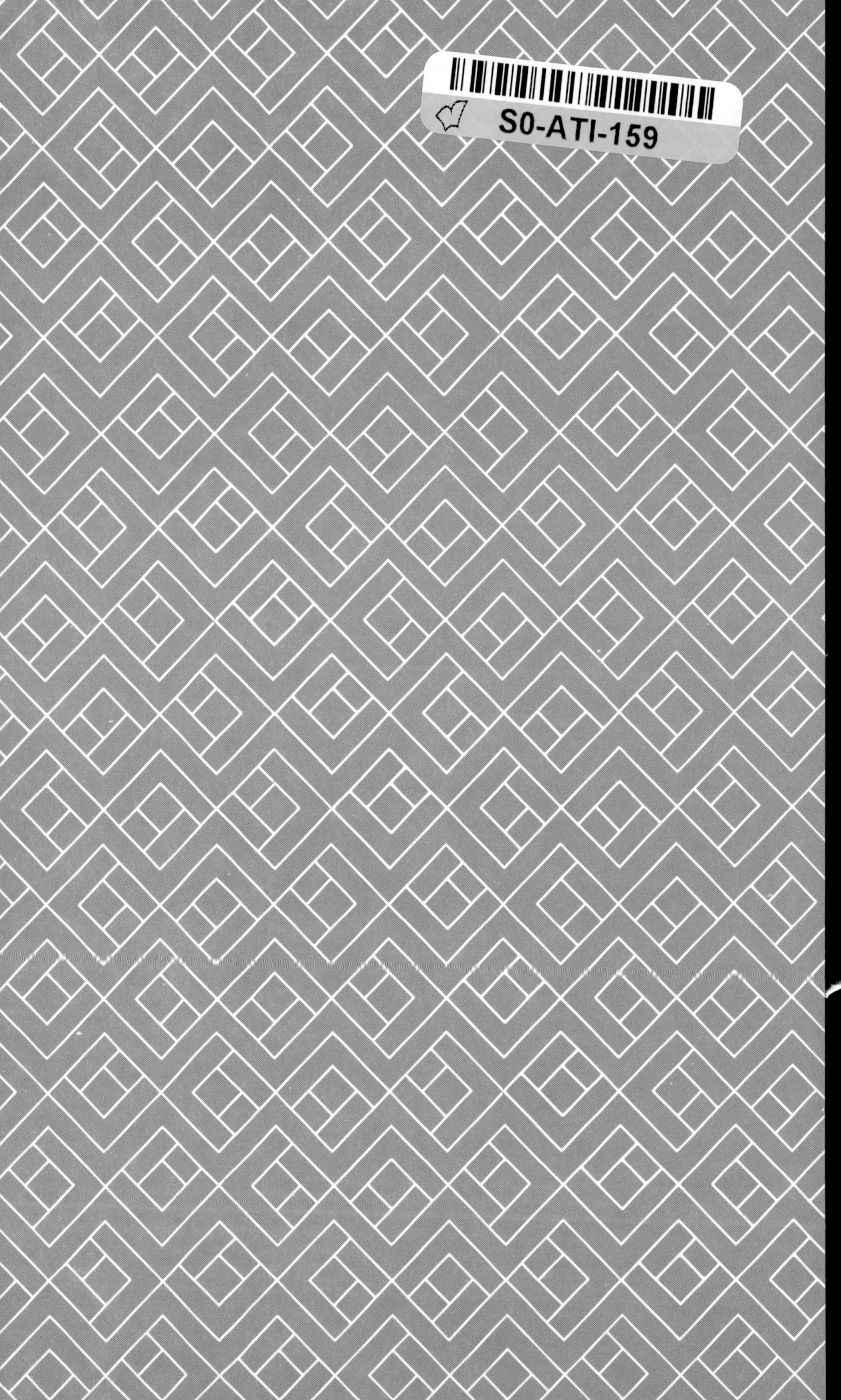
S0-ATI-159

RELATIONS AND REPRESENTATIONS

Relations and Representations is a lucid introduction to the philosophy of social psychological science. John D. Greenwood takes a new and original approach to the subject, repudiating traditional empiricist and hermeneutical accounts. Instead, he advances and defends a realist philosophy of social psychological science that maintains objectivity while at the same time stressing the social dimensions of mind and action.

Dr Greenwood provides novel perspectives on the problems and potential of those sciences concerned with human behaviours that are constituted as meaningful actions by their social relational, and representational dimensions. He focuses in particular on the social identity of human actions and psychological states, on the objectivity of theoretical description and causal explanation, and on the role of experimentation. This approach, aimed at reconciling our scientific interest with our human intuitions, results in a richer conception of social psychological theory and phenomena than is found in most contemporary theoretical accounts.

A stimulating and thought-provoking text, *Relations and Representations* will be of special value to students and teachers of psychology, sociology, anthropology and philosophy.

RELATIONS AND REPRESENTATIONS

An introduction to the philosophy of social psychological science

John D. Greenwood

London and New York

First published in 1991
by Routledge
11 New Fetter Lane, London EC4P 4EE

Simultaneously published in the USA and Canada
by Routledge
a division of Routledge, Chapman and Hall Inc.
29 West 35th Street, New York, NY 10001

Typeset by Michael Mepham, Frome, Somerset
Printed in Great Britain by Mackays of Chatham PLC, Kent.

British Library Cataloguing in Publication Data
Greenwood, J. D. (John Derek) *1952–*
Relations and representations : an introduction to the philosophy of social psychological science.
1. Social psychology
I. Title
302

Library of Congress Cataloging in Publication Data
Greenwood, John D.
Relations and representations: an introduction to the philosophy of social psychological science/John D. Greenwood
p. cm.
Includes bibliographical references and index.
1. Social psychology—Methodology. 2. Social psychology—Philosophy. 3. Social interaction. I. Title.
HM251.G7524 1991
302'.01—dc20 90-47906
CIP

ISBN 0-415-05514-8
0-415-05515-6 (pbk)

For Bill and Nancy Hutcheson

CONTENTS

PREFACE

This short volume aims to provide an introduction to the philosophy of social psychological science. Although primarily directed towards practitioners and students of academic social psychology, it is intended to be rather broader in scope. For it aims to provide an introduction to the philosophy of all sciences concerned with the study of human *actions*, defined as those behaviours that are intentionally (or purposively) directed and socially located. Consequently the discussion is also held to have significant implications for psychology in general, and for the related disciplines of sociology and anthropology.

This volume differs from standard introductions in two important respects. First, most introductions to the philosophy of social psychological science assume the correctness of the standard *empiricist* account of natural science, and then discuss the possibilities and difficulties of applying this model to the social psychological domain. This volume does not assume this. On the contrary, the empiricist account is shown to be hopelessly inadequate, and an alternative *realist* account is recommended in its place. Thus this little volume is also an introduction to a realist philosophy of social psychological science.

Second, this volume makes no attempt to effect a compromise between the extremes of 'scientific' psychology and 'hermeneutical' psychology. The most extreme forms of 'scientific' psychology restrict social psychological science to the explanation, prediction, and control of 'observable behaviour'. The most extreme forms of 'hermeneutical' psychology restrict social psychological science to the explication of the meaning of human action. Most philosophical analyses of social psychological science either adopt one of these opposing positions, or try to achieve some form of integration or reconciliation. This volume does neither. This is because both these positions assume the correctness of the empiricist account of science. The 'scientific' psychologist mistakenly attempts to map the empiricist account onto the social psychological domain. The 'hermeneutical' psychologist appeals to irrelevant contrasts between social psychological science and the empiricist account of science. Since, according to the arguments of this volume, the empiricist account of science is hopelessly inadequate, there is no point in trying to defend either position or effect any reconciliation.

Rather, the present work tries to make a fresh start from the quite different and ideologically neutral perspective of a realist philosophy of science. It consequently focuses on the real issues and difficulties generated by the differences in the *types of object* studied by the natural and social psychological sciences: for human actions, unlike most physical phenomena, are meaningful in nature, and are constituted by their social relational and representational dimensions. Thus the title: 'Relations and Representations'. This volume is a short but sustained attempt to assess the problems and potential of sciences concerned with those human behaviours that are constituted as meaningful actions by their social relational and representational dimensions.

The conclusion of this little volume is optimistic. From a realist perspective one is not forced into a Hobson's choice of the sterilities of 'scientific' psychology or the relativism of 'hermeneutical' psychology. It is argued that from a realist perspective there are no in-principle impediments to objective causal and experimental sciences of meaningful human action, and that most of the traditional methodological (and moral) problems are misconceived. Whether the arguments amount to mere optimism or a substantive alternative to traditional accounts, I leave the reader to judge. My only hope is that any reader will get a broader picture via a consideration of the alternative perspective sketched herein.

I have endeavoured to keep the discussion short and simple in order not to bury the central points and principles under pages of detailed arguments, qualifications, and references. For those stimulated to pursue the issues I raise, a more detailed defence can be found in my monographs *Explanation and Experiment in Social Psychological Science* (1988) and *Personal Identity and the Social Dimensions of Mind* (1991).

This book owes a lot to many people. My greatest debt is to Rom Harré and Paul Secord. I have also profited greatly through discussion and correspondence with Roy Bhaskar, Nicholas Capaldi, Chong Kim Chong, Jerry Ginsburg, James and Diana Herbert, K.D. Irani, Jarrett Leplin, Cheryl Logan, Richard McDonough, Peter Manicas, Joseph Margolis, Glyn Owen, Harry Purser, Martin Tamny, Vicky Tartter, Ralph Rosnow, John Sabini, Michael Tay, Cecilia Wee, and Mabel Wong. I also owe thanks to David Stonestreet, the Psychology Editor at Routledge, and Mary Ann Kernan, the former Psychology Editor at Methuen. Finally I have to thank Shelagh, Robert, and Holly for going on holiday without their husband and father, and apologise to them. Without their sad cooperation this book would never have been written.

This book also owes a lot to my previous publications. In addition to the two monographs mentioned above, I have appropriated, modified, and transformed arguments originally published in *Philosophy of Science*, *Philosophy of Social Science*, *European Journal of Social Psychology*, *Journal for the Theory of Social Behaviour*, *Theoretical and Philosophical Psychology*, *Theory and Psychology*, *New Ideas in Psychology*, and *Social Epistemology*.

I don't expect many people to agree with these arguments. I do hope that many find them challenging.

John D. Greenwood
New York, 1991

INTRODUCTION: SCIENCE AND SCIENTISM

Much of the historical debate about the nature and potential of social psychological science has been a rather confused product of what may be described as the 'me and Newton' syndrome. Since at least the eighteenth century (and especially this century), those concerned to advance and develop social psychological science have self-consciously modelled their research upon what they believe to be the practice of the physical sciences. Unfortunately they have focused almost exclusively upon physics, and the physics of the Newtonian world-view, ignoring the alternative conceptual possibilities suggested by other sciences and contemporary physics. Equally unfortunately they have modelled their research not upon the actual practice of physical science, but upon a particular empiricist account of science that had its origin in philosophical reflections upon Newtonian physics, but which has been largely abandoned by contemporary philosophers of science. Somewhat ironically, the only forms of science that appear to be actually governed by these empiricist principles are those forms of social psychological science that have embraced them.

There is of course nothing wrong *per se* with the attempt by social psychological sciences to emulate the successful achievements of physical sciences by trying to emulate their principles and methods. Indeed they have to do this if such disciplines are to be deserving of the title science. There are those who complain that this is precisely the problem: that human agents and their actions are not appropriate objects of scientific study. It is often claimed that to treat persons as scientific objects dehumanizes them; that the attempt to provide causal explanations of their actions treats them as mechanical automatons rather than free agents; and that to investigate their actions in artificial laboratory experiments generates purely artifactual behaviours that have no explanatory bearing upon human actions in real-life contexts. However, none of these features is intrinsic to a scientific analysis of human agents and their actions. The real distortions to be found in social psychological science derive not from a scientific approach but from a *scientistic* one: the attempt to force social psychological science to adopt principles that are characteristic of particular sciences at particular historical periods, but which are not essential features of science *per se*, and which may be quite inappropriate in the realm of social psychological science.

WHAT IS SCIENCE?

This suggestion presupposes that one has a clear idea as to the nature of science itself. This is a matter of controversy about which a whole book could be written, and I do not pretend to offer a fully adequate or comprehensive definition in this short work. However, it is possible to discriminate certain features that may plausibly be regarded as necessary or essential features: features without which any discipline would not deserve to be described as scientific. It is also possible to identify features that are incidental and non-essential: features that are characteristic of particular sciences at particular historical periods, but without which a discipline could still deserve to be described as scientific. It is a significant and non-accidental fact that those features that may be identified as essential may be best characterized as properties of intellectual disciplines, and that those features that may be identified as non-essential may be best characterized as presumed properties of the *objects* studied by intellectual disciplines.

The arguments of this volume are based upon the assumption that all empirical (as opposed to mathematical) sciences have all three of the following features.

1 *They are objective.* The descriptions and explanations advanced by scientific disciplines are true or false according to whether reality does or does not have the properties attributed to it by these descriptions and explanations.
2 *They advance causal explanations.* The explanations advanced by scientific disciplines provide explanations of how certain events or regularities or structures are produced or generated.
3 *They employ observational methods.* The observational methods

employed by sciences enable scientists to discriminate causal factors and evaluate competing causal explanations.

It will be argued in this volume that social psychological science can satisfy all these criteria. Some radical theorists deny this, claiming that social psychological science cannot in principle satisfy them, and that it is inappropriate to require that it should. It will be argued that such claims are not well grounded.

There are four principles that are often held to be essential features of science, but in fact are not. These are as follows.

The principle of atomism. A commitment to the principle that the phenomena studied can be individuated and exist independently of other phenomena to which they may be related. This principle is of course a cornerstone of Newtonian science, and underpins a great many highly successful scientific theories (e.g. the atomic theory, the periodic table, etc.). It continues to dominate much physical science and many branches of social psychological science.

Nevertheless atomism involves a commitment to an assumption about reality that is not an intrinsic feature of scientific thought. Modern physics has remained successful while abandoning commitment to this principle: the nature of theoretical entities such as electromagnetic fields and quarks seems to be determined (at least in part) by their relational location. Thus it is an open question whether this principle applies to social psychological phenomena. It will be argued in this work that it does not.

The universality of causal explanation. The principle that properly scientific explanations are universal in their application: that the same explanation applies to each and every instance of a given event, regularity, or structure. The principle may be alternatively expressed as the principle of the *singularity of causation*: that every event, regularity, or structure has (at least on some level of description) one and only one causal explanation. However, although this principle does appear to hold true with respect to many physical phenomena, it does not appear to hold true with respect to them all. Thus although there appears to be (ultimately) only one cause of death, rusting, and superconductivity, there appear to be a plurality of causes of some diseases (some cancers appear to be induced by external agents, others are the product of genetic inheritance). Consequently it is an open question whether this principle applies to social psychological phenomena. It will be argued in this work that it cannot be presumed to apply to them.

It is most unfortunate that this principle is restrictively applied in social psychological science as some sort of criterion for the adequacy of an explanation. For the restrictive application of this principle seems to be derived from a misunderstanding of the supposedly paradigmatic form of scientific explanation advanced by the Newtonian theory of universal gravitation. According to this theory, all physical bodies in the universe are subject to gravitational forces. It does not follow, however, nor is it in fact the case, that the motions of all physical bodies must or can be explained in terms of gravitational forces. The motions of some bodies must and can be explained in terms of electromagnetic forces.

The principle of ontological invariance in space and time. The principle that the entities studied by science can be re-identified across different regions of space and time is a presupposition of the Newtonian theory of universal gravitation, and it seems clear that it applies to many of the phenomena studied by astronomy, subatomic physics, and chemistry (e.g. planets, electrons, and acids). It seems equally clear that it does not apply to many of the phenomena studied by evolutionary biology and medicine (e.g. species and viruses). It is thus an open question whether this principle applies to social psychological phenomena. It will be argued in this work that it cannot be presumed to apply to them.

The principle of causal determinism. The principle that for every event there is a set of antecedent factors whose conjunction is ontologically sufficient to produce that event when they are instantiated, and a description of which is logically sufficient for the successful prediction of that event, is a presupposition of Newton's theory of universal gravitation, well-known for its impressive predictive achievements. This principle has, however, been abandoned by contemporary quantum physics.

It is often thought that this principle is a necessary presupposition of any form of science, that it is a condition of experimentation, and that it precludes the possibility of human agency or freedom. However, although the practice of science and experimentation does presuppose that every event has a causal explanation, this principle of universal causal explanation is logically distinct from the principle of universal causal determinism. The two principles are only identifiable given a particular and restrictive empiricist account of causality in terms of invariant sequence. They are not identifiable given a realist account of causality in terms of powerful particulars, for this leaves open the possibility that some (human) powers that are referenced in causal explanations of human action may be under the control of some (human) agents.

A commitment to any or all of these principles is not an intrinsic feature of science. In consequence it may be argued that it is inappropriate to treat them as requirements for social psychological science, or to consider that such a discipline is somehow deficient or unscientific because it fails to satisfy them. Many of the justified complaints about contemporary social psychological science are directed not towards its status as a science, but its frequent treatment of commitment to such principles as the *sine qua non* of science.

EXPERIMENTATION

There is one feature that, although not essential to science, is clearly desirable. This is the employment of *experimentation*: the ability to create, through intervention, situations that enable observers to isolate causal factors and evaluate competing causal explanations. This is plainly not an essential feature of science, since astronomy and geology have managed notable theoretical achievements without it. Causal factors can be discriminated and competing causal explanations evaluated by a comparative analysis of naturally occurring systems. Nevertheless the ability to intervene and control hypothetical causal factors does clearly furnish many experimental sciences with an extremely powerful resource that is exploited whenever and wherever possible.

It should be noted, however, that there are two features characteristic of experimentation, only one of which can be presumed to apply in the case of social psychological science. The first is the ability to intervene and create situations that might not arise naturally. This is of course possible in social psychological science, although there are limits (both practical and moral). The second is the ability to isolate the phenomena under investigation from other factors. It is much less obvious that this second feature applies in the case of social psychological science, since it presumes the applicability of the principle of atomism. It has already been noted that it is an open question whether this principle applies to social psychological phenomena, and that it is argued in this work that it does not. It will also be argued that this generates very real problems with respect to the employment of experimentation in social psychological science.

MEANING EMPIRICISM

There is one other principle, commitment to which is often held to be an essential feature of science. This is the so-called *principle of empiricism*. Now in one respect this claim is utterly uncontentious, for in one respect this claim is trivially true. If commitment to this principle just means that scientific theories ought to be adjudicated in terms of the empirically discriminable evidence available to scientists, then it is innocuous. This is simply the testability requirement noted above as the third essential feature of science. In this respect all scientists are empiricists, or ought to be.

However, this is not the only fashion in which this principle is interpreted. The most extreme interpretation is given by behaviourism, according to which social psychological science is restricted to the explanation of observables (behaviour) by reference to other observables (environmental stimuli and learning history). Any reference to theoretical entities that are 'unobservable' is rejected as illegitimate. This extreme interpretation is of course alien to most sciences, including physics, which cheerfully progresses by employing explanations couched in terms of 'unobservables' such as electromagnetic force and proton donation.

Only slightly less extreme but enormously influential is the doctrine that theoretical references to 'unobservables' – such as motives and asymmetric social structures – must be operationally defined in terms of observables. It is worth stressing that this doctrine is almost unique to social psychological science. One would have to look long and hard to find anything in a physics or biology text remotely resembling an operational definition of an electron or nerve cell. Percy Bridgeman (1927), the Nobel physicist who gave this doctrine its name and convinced many social psychological scientists to adopt it, failed to convince most of his natural-science colleagues.

This special interpretation of the principle of empiricism may be classified as the principle of *meaning empiricism*. According to this principle, a concept or its linguistic expression in a description is meaningful if and only if it can be defined in terms of observables, either by an ostensive definition (by pointing to a sample of the objects referenced by the concept or description) or an operational definition (by defining the concept or its linguistic expression in terms of concepts or descriptions that can be defined ostensively).

The origin of this influential doctrine is not difficult to trace. It derives from the classical empiricist account of concept formation and word meaning, developed by the empiricist philosophers Locke (1690), Berkeley (1710), and Hume (1739). Central to this account is the assumption that sensation and cognition are essentially *homogeneous*. Locke, Berkeley, and Hume held that 'ideas' (thoughts, concepts, etc.) are 'copies' or 'faint images' of 'sense impressions'. They differ from them in degree but not in kind ('ideas' have less 'force and liveliness' than 'sense impressions'). In consequence the sense experience of an X was held to be a necessary condition for the meaningful employment of the concept of an X. Thus a blind man was said to be unable to form the concept of redness. Since it was also held that linguistic descriptions derive their meaning by mental association with 'ideas', the sense experience of an X was held to be a necessary condition for the meaningful employment of the linguistic description 'X'. Thus a blind man was said to be unable to grasp the meaning of the linguistic description 'red'. In the twentieth century this account of linguistic meaning was appropriated and developed by logical positivists and scientific empiricists into the 'verification principle' for the meaning of factual propositions: 'The meaning of a proposition is the method of its verification' (Schlick 1936: 148).

Commitment to this principle continues to inform much contemporary debate about the scientific status of social psychological science, and creates conceptual havoc in social psychological theory and research. It is worth noting at this stage that the original premiss of the empiricist account – the assumption of the homogeneity of sensation and cognition – is now rejected by most psychologists and philosophers. Although some contemporary cognitive psychologists argue that some forms of cognitive and linguistic processing involve the employment of images (Paivio 1986), all have abandoned the notion that cognitions are to be conceptually identified with images, and that linguistic expressions derive their meaning by association with images (Simon and Kaplan 1989). None I know would even defend the view that images are necessary for cognitive and linguistic processing, and a good many straightforwardly deny this (Pylyshyn 1984). Philosophers these days are also moved to stress the important differences between cognition and sensation (Margolis 1984; Rorty 1979), between for example our thought that the table is red and our sense experience of redness. Our thoughts have meaningful contents that are intentional: our thought that the table is red is 'about' the table. Our sensations do not: our sensation of redness has no meaningful content and is not 'about' anything.

Consequently there is no longer any good reason for maintaining the principle of meaning empiricism. As shall be noted in the following chapters, there are also very good reasons for rejecting it.

OBJECTIVITY

One particular negative consequence of commitment to the principle of meaning empiricism is worth mentioning in advance. The doctrine that theoretical terms must be defined in terms of 'observables' leads to the regular confusion of questions in debates about the objectivity of social psychological science. In particular it promotes the confounding of quite separate questions about the *linguistic* and *epistemic* objectivity of social psychological science.

The question of *linguistic objectivity* concerns the truth conditions of linguistic descriptions. A description may be said to be *linguistically objective* if it is true or false according to whether or not the reality putatively described exists and has or has not the properties or relations attributed to it by the description. On this criterion all the following descriptive claims may be said to be linguistically objective: 'This table is rectangular'; 'Elements are composed of atoms'; 'God is just'; '7 is greater than 5'; 'Abortion is morally wrong'.

Notice that for a description to be linguistically objective it is not necessary that its truth or falsity can be established by reference to observations. 'This table is rectangular' is true if and only if the particular item referenced has the properties of a table (if it is a piece of furniture with a horizontal frame and flat upper surface supported by legs etc.) and has a rectangular shape, and this can be confirmed by observation. 'Seven is greater than 5' is true if and only if the number seven has a greater numerical value than five, but this cannot be established by any form of observation, although it can be established by reference to the axioms and recursive rules of arithmetic. Notice also that according to this criterion it is not even necessary that the truth or falsity of a descriptive claim is capable of being established by *any* form of observational evidence or logical grounds. 'God is just' is true if and only if there exists an entity that has the constitutive properties of God according to some definition (omnipotence, omniscience, etc.) and is also just. This claim may be true or false even if we have no observational or logical means of evaluating its truth or falsity.

The employment of a linguistically objective description – or representation of reality informed by such a description – is neither a necessary nor sufficient condition of the truth of the proposition expressed by it. Thus the descriptions 'Elements are composed of atoms' and 'God is just' are true or false irrespective of whether anyone employs these descriptions, or represents reality in terms of them.

A description may be said to be *linguistically subjective* if its employment – or a representation of reality informed by such a description – is a necessary or sufficient condition of its truth. Convincing candidates are in fact hard to find, but something like this appears to be true of the following cases. Descriptive claims about how things seem to individuals may be said to be linguistically subjective. It would appear to be a necessary and sufficient condition of the truth of 'It seems warm in here', 'I seem to see a blue patch in my visual field', and (arguably) 'It feels painful' that the individual concerned judges that it seems warm to her, that she seems to see a blue patch, and that it feels painful. Her linguistically informed judgements that it seems warm to her, that she seems to see a blue patch, and that it feels painful, may be said to be wholly or at least partially *constitutive* of its seeming warm to her, her seeming to see a blue patch, and its feeling painful to her. In contrast, it is not a necessary or sufficient condition of the truth of the descriptive claims that 'Elements are composed of atoms' and 'God is just' that anyone makes these judgements, and such judgements by individuals or social collectives are not in any way constitutive of the composition of elements or the existence and properties of God.

Perhaps the best way to illustrate this difference is by reference to the historical debate about the linguistic status of moral discourse. Many traditional moral theorists such as John Stuart Mill assumed that moral discourse is descriptive and linguistically objective, and that the proper area of disputation concerned the correct theoretical definition of terms such as moral 'goodness' or 'rightness'. According to a grossly simplified statement of Mill's (1863) own utilitarian account, an action is morally good if it maximizes human happiness and minimizes human misery. According to this conception, it is an entirely objective question whether any action is morally good. It entirely depends upon whether or not it maximizes human happiness and minimizes human misery, however easy or difficult it is to make an estimate of its consequences in terms of human happiness or misery. The moral worth of an action is not constituted in whole or in part by the judgement of any individual or social collective that it is morally good. Such judgements will be straightforwardly false if the action does not maximize human happiness and minimize human misery, no matter how strongly committed individuals or social collectives are to its truth.

In contrast, during the early part of the twentieth century, many moral theorists denied that moral discourse is descriptive of moral facts about the world. According to the 'emotive' analysis of moral discourse advanced by Stevenson (1944), to claim that an action is morally good is just to judge that one approves of it. An individual's judgement that an action is morally good is constitutive of the moral value of that action for that individual. This is because judging that one approves of an action is a necessary and sufficient condition of approving of that action. According to the 'relativist' analysis of moral discourse advanced by Herskovits (1948), to claim that an action is morally good is just to claim that it is approved by the majority of members of a society (or the majority of authorities or powerful members, or some such variant). The judgement of the goodness of a form of action by the majority of members of a society is constitutive of the moral worth of a form of action for members of that society. This is because the judgement of the majority that they approve of a form of action is a necessary and sufficient condition of their approval.

According to these linguistically subjective accounts of moral discourse, claims about the moral worth of actions are not true or false independently of the judgements of individuals or social collectives, since actions cannot be approved by individuals or social collectives independently of their judgements of approval.

In contrast, many contemporary moral theorists have returned to a form of 'realism' (Sayre-McCord 1989) about moral discourse. According to this account actions have moral value independently of the judgements of particular individuals or social collectives.

According to this account the judgement of an individual that child pornography is morally acceptable may be simply false, no matter how strongly the individual feels that it is morally acceptable. According to this account the judgement of the majority of members of a society that capital punishment is morally required may be simply false, no matter how many members are strongly committed to this judgement. Such actions may be characterized as morally wrong on grounds independent of the judgements of individuals or social collectives: because, for example, they violate the rights of children, or because of the omnipresent possibility that an executed person may be innocent of any crime.

The question of *epistemic objectivity* is quite distinct from the question of linguistic objectivity. The employment of a description may be said to be *epistemically objective* if its truth or falsity can be determined or evaluated by observational evidence (in the case of empirical sciences) or rational grounds (in mathematics, religion, and (arguably) morality). Since no scientist would claim that any theoretical claim can be established with certainty, and since this requirement has long been abandoned by philosophers, we may say that the employment of theoretical descriptions – in the case of empirical sciences – is epistemologically objective if it is possible to evaluate them by means of observational evidence: if such evidence provides rational grounds for preferring one theoretical description over others. If it is not possible in principle to do so, if such evidence cannot in principle provide rational grounds for preferring one theoretical description over others, then the employment of such descriptions may be said to be *epistemically subjective*. Their employment can only be governed by the vagaries of individual psychological preferences or social, economic, or political forces, etc.

It is critical to stress that these forms of objectivity are logically distinct, because they are so regularly confounded as a consequence of frequent commitment to the principle of meaning empiricism. Thus at one extreme the empiricist holds that epistemic objectivity can be preserved only if theoretical claims are operationally defined in terms of observables, because this is held to be a condition of their testability. It shall be noted in the following chapters that this view is utterly mistaken. At the other extreme, the social constructionist theorist holds that doubts about the epistemic objectivity of social psychological theories casts doubt upon their linguistic objectivity. It shall also be noted that this view is utterly mistaken.

These claims are defended in the following chapters. There it will be argued that as a matter of fact theoretical descriptions in social psychological science are both linguistically and epistemically objective.

EXPLANATION AND UNDERSTANDING

One final point. As should be clear from these introductory remarks, I see no reason why disciplines concerned with the evaluation of causal explanations of human action should not be properly described as scientific disciplines. This commitment does not of course preclude recognition of the special features of social psychological science that may be required to accommodate the special features of social psychological phenomena.

Human actions, unlike many other physical events, are meaningful and purposive. There are of course many this century, from Watson (1924) and Skinner (1953) to Churchland (1979) and Stich (1983), who would argue that meaning and purpose have no more place in social psychological science than they have in contemporary physics and biology. Indeed they argue that social and psychological sciences will only become scientific when, like post-Galilean physics and post-Darwinian biology, they also eliminate all reference to meaning and purpose.

The case for this argument with respect to social psychological science is much less secure than it was with respect to physics and biology. Our theoretical attribution of meaning and purpose to the motions of physical bodies (in Aristotelean physics) and biological development (in vitalist biology) was modelled upon the paradigm case of the explanation of human action, where references to meaning and purpose seem essential to their best explanation. We have come to believe (with justification) that this theoretical model is inappropriate for physics and biology. Our best explanations of the motions of physical bodies and biological development do not appear to require any reference to meaning and purpose. The case is, however, notably different with respect to social psychological science. It is far from obvious that meaning and purpose are eliminable from our best explanations of human action. Certainly there are no universally or consensually accepted theories of human action that presently have this feature. Nor does the eliminability of meaning and purpose from social psychological science follow from its successful elimination from physics and biology. The inappropriateness of extending explanations successful in one domain to others via theoretical modelling never establishes the inaccuracy of such explanations in their original domain. No scientist who rejects the wave theory of light feels obliged or inclined to reject the wave theory of waves.

One of the central themes of this work is that social psychological science, like any other branch of science, is concerned to advance causal explanations. However, its aim is not and cannot be restricted to causal explanation. For social psychological science, unlike many other sciences, must also aim to gain *understanding* of the *meaning* of the phenomena it studies. This is not to claim with the 'hermeneutical psychologist' (Gauld and Shotter 1977) that understanding the meaning of human action is a more appropriate substitute for or alternative to causal explanation. It is to claim that a proper understanding of the meaning of human action is a prerequisite for the scientific evaluation of causal explanations of human action.

1

SOCIAL DIMENSIONS OF ACTION

It is often stated that the goal of social psychological science is the explanation, prediction, and control of human *behaviour*, defined in terms of observable physical movements. Yet as a matter of fact most practitioners are not much concerned with behaviour *per se*, but rather aim to provide empirically-supported theoretical explanations of *socially meaningful* behaviours such as aggression, dishonesty, marriage breakdown, destructive obedience, suicide, helping others, etc. These *forms of action* cannot be equated with the physical dimensions of behaviour, for forms of action such as aggression and dishonesty can be manifested by means of an infinite variety of physical behaviours. Definitions of actions in terms of their physical dimensions would include too much and too little. For example, definitions of aggression in terms of arm movements would include warnings and auction bids, and exclude acts of aggression by poisoning and the use of electric shock generators.

This basic point can be made very simply. A person may make all sorts of physical movements and noises, but few of these movements or noises will count as human actions unless they are intentionally directed and socially located: that is, unless they have some represented purpose for the participating agent and have social significance according to the local conventions of contexts of action. Thus, for example, my arm waving only counts as an 'all-clear' signal if it is represented by me as directed towards the communication of this message and if it exploits an agreed convention about the meaning of such arm waving in certain social contexts. Analogously a piece of behaviour only counts as an act of obedience if the person who obeys represents his behaviour as the following of an order and if the person who issues the order is in a social position to do so.

THE SOCIAL CONSTITUTION OF ACTION

Diverse physical behaviours are constituted as forms of action by their intentional direction and social location. Most human actions may be said to be *socially constituted* in the following respects. Behaviours are constituted as diverse forms of action by *social relations* and by *participant agent representations* and *collective representations* of behaviour.

Social relations

Many actions and social practices are relational in nature. Behaviours are constituted as actions and social practices by their location in social relational contexts. Thus for example a trial by jury is constituted (in part) as a trial by jury by its legitimizing relations to legal, judicial, and penal systems. An employment interview is constituted (in part) as an employment interview by relations of authorization with respect to the organization within which it is located.

This marks an important difference between most of the phenomena studied by the natural sciences and social psychological sciences. Most of the phenomena studied by natural sciences such as physics and chemistry are logically *atomistic* in nature: their *identity* is determined by their *intrinsic* composition and structure. Thus for example an acid is defined as a solution with a high concentration of hydrogen ions; copper is defined as an element with atomic number 29 and atomic weight 63.54. Accordingly an acid or sample of copper retains its identity as an acid or sample of copper in isolation from other physical phenomena.

In contrast many human actions and social practices are logically non-atomistic and *relational* in nature: their identity is determined by their relation to phenomena *extrinsic* to them. Thus behaviours do not count as acts of obedience and marriage outside of the appropriate institutional contexts in which they occur. Behaviours do not count as acts of sentencing or interviewing in isolation from appropriate social settings.

This is not to deny that many social psychological phenomena are also constituted by *intrinsic* relations. An employment interview for example is also partially constituted by the intrinsic relations between interviewer(s) and interviewee(s). It is rather to stress that a great many actions and practices are *also* constituted by relations to phenomena that are *extrinsic* to them.[1] Thus for example a trial by jury is constituted both by the relations between participants (judge, jurors, defendant, legal counsel, etc.) and its relation to legal, judicial, and penal systems. A group of agents cannot willy-nilly join together to constitute a trial by jury or employment interview by arbitrarily designating some persons as jurors, defendant, interviewer, etc. These social phenomena should be contrasted with the constitution of a party, for example, which is wholly constituted as a party by intrinsic relations between participants. Thus any group of persons at any place and time can join together and have a party.

It might be objected that the supposed contrast between the objects studied by natural and social psychological sciences is strained, for it might be objected that physical entities are frequently defined in terms of their relation to other physical entities, and that this is a characteristic feature of any scientific system of linguistic classification. Thus protons and electrons are defined in terms of their opposing positive and negative electric charges; acids and alkalis are defined in terms of their respective concentrations of hydrogen and hydroxyl ions (their pH values).

However, this would be to miss the point of the contrast, and confuses the relational nature of the meaning of classificatory descriptions with the relational nature of phenomena themselves. The basic point may be illustrated in the following fashion. Although the meanings of most classificatory descriptions in natural and social psychological science are interdefined and in this respect may be said to be relational in nature, most physical phenomena such as protons and acids are non-relational and atomistic because they can exist individually *in isolation* from other physical phenomena such as electrons and alkalis. In contrast, social psychological phenomena such as trials by jury and interviews are relational and non-atomistic because they cannot exist independently of their relational location. If a set of behaviours do not bear the appropriate institutional relations, they are not instances of trial by jury or employment interview.

Participant agent representations

Social relations are rarely sufficient to constitute behaviours as forms of action. It is not sufficient for a trial by jury that individuals gather together in a courtroom and adopt the roles of judge, juror, counsel, etc., and that their behaviours maintain the appropriate legitimizing relations to legal, judicial, and penal systems. Their behaviours must also be purposively directed to assessing evidence concerning the guilt of the defendant.

A great many behaviours are also constituted as actions by participant agent representations of the intentional direction of the behaviour: that is, the point and purpose of the behaviour as represented by the person engaged in it. Thus for example a wide variety of physically diverse behaviours – raising an arm, moving a switch on a shock generator, putting poison in another's coffee – are constituted as acts of aggression by being represented by the participating agent as directed towards the injury of another. A wide variety of physically diverse behaviours – keeping the wrong change, removing goods from a store without payment, etc. – are constituted as dishonest actions by being represented by participating agents as involving the removal or receipt of goods or services that rightly (according to some moral convention) belong to another.

Now these forms of action may be said to be socially constituted in two respects. The first is that the contents of some participant agent representations are products of social conventions that have been grasped by participating agents. Dishonest actions can only occur in forms of social life that have socially recognized rules governing the ownership of property. The second is that the meaningful contents of many of the representational states we attribute to humans are appropriated from the meaningful contents of language, which is itself a social construction or creation. Jury decisions and prayers can only occur in forms of social life whose language enables agents to represent some of their behaviours as directed towards the assessment of evidence concerning the guilt of a defendant and directed towards communication with a supreme being. Non-linguistic animals may be described as engaged in violent behaviour, but not aggressive actions: they lack the linguistic resources necessary to represent their behaviours as directed towards the injury of others.[2]

Such participant agent representations are sometimes sufficient to constitute a behaviour as a form of action, as in the examples of aggression and dishonesty. They are not always sufficient. As noted above, it is not enough to represent one's behaviour in appropriate ways for it to constitute the actions of interviewers or jurors: these behaviours must also occur in the appropriate social locations. On the other hand they are frequently necessary. Behaviours only count as acts of aggression, dishonesty, employment, interviewing, and sentencing if they are represented by agents in the appropriate ways. They are not, however, always necessary. Some behaviours are constituted as actions quite independently of the participating agent's representation of their point and purpose. Thus I may unintentionally insult my colleagues or foreign guests by my neglect of their considerable achievements or by trying to attract their attention by crooking my forefinger (an extreme insult in some Asian cultures). These behaviours need not be represented by me as affronts to the dignity of others for the behaviours to be insults.

Collective representations

A great many behaviours are constituted as actions by collective representations of the social significance of certain forms of behaviour according to a local convention. Certain behaviours, for example, are constituted as insults and obligations by being conventionally represented by members of a social collective as offensive to another's dignity and as a social commitments. There is no requirement that participating agents represent their behaviours or situation as offensive to another's dignity or involving a social commitment. Thus an agent may insult another even if neither person recognizes that the behaviour is a conventional affront to another's dignity. A man may be morally or financially indebted to another even if neither recognizes that this is the case. Of course many potential observers must conventionally represent such forms of behaviour as offensive to another's dignity and as social commitments for there to be forms of insult and obligation in any form of social life. However, it is not necessary in any particular case that participating agents recognize the significance of their actions. Thus the socially inept will often unintentionally insult their friends and colleagues, and the unwary anthropologist may mortally offend the family of the tribal king by refusing to eat human flesh.

Now most of these points about the social dimensions of human actions ought to be uncontroversial and obvious to any socially competent person, for they are embedded in the logic of our everyday thought and discourse about human action. However, they are not treated as obvious but rather as extremely problematic by most practitioners of social psychological science. One reason for this is the traditional empiricist obsession with the 'observable': many researchers want to restrict scientific analysis to 'observable behaviour' only. In Chapter 4 it will be argued that there is no justification for this peculiar dogma, and it is certainly not a view commonly held by practitioners of the 'hard' physical sciences.

At present it is sufficient to note again that social psychological scientists do not so restrict their analysis. They regularly avow explanations of socially meaningful *actions* such as helping others, play, cooperation, and suicide. Insofar as they do so they *must* be concerned to establish that the social relations and representations that constitute diverse behaviours as forms of action are present with respect to the particular actions that are the focus of their particular empirical and experimental enquiries. Otherwise their avowed explanations will not be empirically supported as explanations of helping others, play, cooperation, suicide, etc. Thus, for example, unless it is established that experimental behaviours satisfy the social relational and representational requirements for obedience, explanatory inferences based upon such experiments cannot be presumed to furnish explanations of the socially meaningful behaviours that are acts of obedience.

CONSTITUTION AND CLASSIFICATION

One reason why many researchers are disinclined to admit that human actions and social practices are constituted by social relations and representations is because they feel that this would somehow mean that the explanatory domain of social psychological science is irreducibly subjective, and therefore an inappropriate object of scientific analysis.

Now in one trivial respect it is of course true to say that the explanatory domain of social psychological science is irreducibly subjective, insofar as it is concerned with the actions and practices of human *subjects*. It is also true to say that much of the explanatory domain of social psychological science does not exist independently of representations of it by human subjects. This marks an important ontological difference between the entities of social psychological and natural sciences, for the entities investigated by natural sciences such as physics and chemistry do exist independently of human representations of them. There could be no acts of aggression if there were no human agents to represent their behaviours as directed towards the injury of others, but there would be uniformly accelerating bodies and photosynthetic reactions even if there were no scientists or laypersons to represent physical reality as having these properties.

However, this ontological difference simply marks differences in the constitutive dimensions of social psychological and physical phenomena. Human actions and social practices are constituted by their social relational and representational dimensions. Physical phenomena are constituted by their physical composition and structure. It does not mark any difference with respect to the *objectivity* of our scientific descriptions of them. A classificatory description may be said to be *linguistically objective* if it is true or false according to whether or not the reality putatively described exists and has or has not the properties or relations attributed to it by the description: if it is true or false independently of the employment of the description by individual agents or social collectives.

Our classificatory descriptions of physical phenomena as instances of acids and carbon may be said to be linguistically objective because such descriptions are true or false according to whether the entities concerned have the properties attributed to them by our descriptions. Thus an entity is accurately described as an acid if and only if it is a solution with a high concentration of hydrogen ions. It is neither a necessary nor a sufficient condition of an entity's being an acid that it is described or represented as an 'acid' by scientists. It is necessary and sufficient that it is a solution with a high concentration of hydrogen ions (that it has the properties referenced by our linguistic description 'acid').

Our classificatory descriptions of human actions and social practices are no less objective just because many behaviours are constituted as actions and social practices by participant agent representations of them. Our classificatory descriptions of human actions and social practices are linguistically objective because they are true or false according to whether the phenomena concerned have the properties attributed to them by our descriptions. Thus a behaviour may be accurately described as an act of aggression if and only if it is represented by the participating agent as directed towards the injury of another; a behaviour may be accurately described as a dishonest action if and only if it is represented by the agent as involving the removal or receipt of goods or services that rightly belong to another. It is neither a necessary nor a sufficient condition of an act of aggression or dishonesty that it is described or represented by the participating agent or any observer as an act of 'aggression' or 'dishonesty'. It is necessary and sufficient that the participating agent represents his or her behaviour as directed towards the injury of another or as involving the removal or receipt of goods or services that rightly belong to another (that it has the properties referenced by our linguistic descriptions 'aggression' and 'dishonesty'). Some individuals may simply be mistaken in their judgements that their acts of self-defence or receipt of unsolicited prizes are instances of aggression and dishonesty, and this will be the case whenever their behaviours are not directed towards the injury of another and do not involve the removal or receipt of goods or services that rightly belong to another. Agents may be aggressive and dishonest without recognizing that they are being aggressive and dishonest. Indeed this fact may occasionally serve as an adequate explanation of some instances of aggression and dishonesty.

Precisely the same is true of those behaviours that are constituted as actions and social practices by social relations and conventional collective representations of their social significance. Social practices are accurately described as trials by jury if and only if they are socially located within legitimizing institutions, and if participants represent their behaviours as directed towards the assessment of evidence concerning the guilt of the defendant. It is neither a necessary nor a sufficient condition of the social practice of trial by jury that participant agents or observers describe or represent the social practice as 'trial by jury'. Actions may be accurately described as insults if and only if the form of behaviour involved is conventionally represented by members of a social collective as offensive to another's dignity. It is neither a necessary nor a sufficient condition of insulting another that participant agents or observers describe or represent the action as an 'insult'. The fact that forms of insults and obligations are constituted by collective representations of social significance is of course no guarantee that collectives or individuals will be accurate or consistent in their descriptions or representations of actions as 'insults' and 'obligations'. Thus we may be quick to remind others of their obligations but slow to recognize our own. We may be sensitive to the offenses of other persons and racial groups but oblivious to the offensive nature of our own actions.

The basic point may be expressed in the following fashion. It is not the case that human actions and social practices are in any way constituted *as actions and practices* by our descriptions or linguistically informed representations of them as instances of actions and social practices such as 'trial by jury', 'aggression', and 'insult'. It is the case that human behaviours – in the sense of physical movements – are constituted as actions and social practices by their social relations, and by participant agent and collective representations of their point and purpose and social significance. Our classificatory descriptions of human actions are descriptions of behaviours that may be said to be *preformed* as actions by such social relational and representational dimensions, just as our classificatory descriptions of physical entities are descriptions of entities that may be said to be preformed as physical entities by their physical dimensions. Our descriptions of actions and social practices are true or false according to whether a particular action or social practice has or has not the social relational and representational dimensions attributed to it by a particular description.

Agent representations of their behaviour that are constitutive of human actions are not themselves descriptions – or theoretical interpretations – of their actions. Such representations cannot themselves be characterized as true or false, although they often presuppose beliefs that can be. Thus my representation of my behaviour as directed towards the injury of another that is constitutive of my aggressive action is not itself a description – or theoretical interpretation – of my action. This representation cannot itself be characterized as true or false, although it presupposes certain beliefs that can be (e.g. that my behaviour is likely to cause the other injury).

A number of points perhaps ought to be stressed to avoid possible and perhaps likely misinterpretation. First, to claim that many actions are constituted by participant agent and collective representations is only to claim that many behaviours (or forms of behaviour) are constituted as actions by the meaningful contents of psychological states that are directed upon them. It is not to claim that such psychological states are themselves 'copies' or 'images' or 'reflections' of behaviour or action, or of anything at all. I use the term 'representation' as the most theoretically neutral term I can think of to capture the contentful nature and directionality of such psychological states.

Second, to claim that many human actions are constituted by agent representations of behaviour is not to claim that it is a necessary condition of these actions that the agent is conscious of or can articulate the content of such psychological states, or that the participant agent is any sort of authority with respect to the description of such psychological states. Many agents may *misdescribe* their actions as 'aggressive' or 'dishonest', despite the constitutive role of such psychological states. The degree to which agents and observers can have access to the contents of such psychological states is an important epistemological issue, to which attention will be directed in Chapters 4 and 6. However, as noted in the Introduction, such issues concerning epistemic objectivity are logically distinct from issues of linguistic objectivity. Thus the linguistic objectivity of our descriptions of human actions can be maintained even if we come to accept that it is enormously difficult (or even impossible in principle) to determine their truth or falsity with any reasonable degree of assurance.

Third, to make the above claims about the linguistic objectivity of our descriptions of socially constituted human actions is not to deny or underestimate the degree of social construction and linguistic negotiation involved in the creation of forms of human action and social practices. Acts of sentencing and patriotism do not occur in forms of social life that lack the appropriate social structures and conventions, and may be eliminated from contemporary forms of social life when these structures and conventions change, perhaps as a result of our linguistic reflections upon them. If persons in a form of social life do not endorse or cease to endorse social conventions about property ownership, there will be no dishonest actions in that form of social life, and this may be a product of revolutionary actions informed by linguistic condemnations. Organized religion is a product of social discourse about the existence and properties and moral prescriptions of a supreme being (or beings), and socially negotiated forms of rituals and institutional practices.

This is true and important, but all it shows is that the social relational and representational dimensions of human actions may be different in different forms of social life and may be transformed over historical time, and that this is very often a product of our socially evolved forms of discourse about them, which may be unique to certain cultures or historical periods. It does not demonstrate or even imply that our descriptive discourse about such actions is in any way constitutive of them.

The meaningful contents of our descriptive discourse about human actions are themselves socially constructed and negotiated. It is important to stress, however, that the social dimensions of human actions are logically independent of the social dimensions of our descriptions of them: the social dimensions of human actions are not a logical consequence of the social dimensions of our descriptions of them (or our representations of them informed by such descriptions). The meaningful contents of our descriptive discourse about physical entities such as acids or copper are also socially constructed and negotiated. However, it does not follow, nor is it true to say, that acids and copper have social dimensions.

It is of course true that our employment of descriptions of actions is subject to all sorts of social psychological influences and biases, despite our best intentions to employ these descriptions in accord with the facts of the matter. Precisely the same is also true of our employment of natural scientific descriptions. Some suggest that our employment of such descriptions is always determined by such social psychological influences and biases, and that there is consequently no guarantee that our actual employment of such descriptions is regularly or indeed ever in accord with the 'facts'. This is a counsel of despair that I do not share. Yet even if it were correct, it simply would not follow that our descriptions of actions or physical entities are in any way constitutive of them, given the logical independence of issues of linguistic and epistemic objectivity. The counsel of despair would only oblige us to conclude that we can never know if any actions are truly aggressive or dishonest etc., or that any entities are acids, samples of copper, etc.

Those who make claims about the socio-linguistic constitution of human actions often call themselves *social constructionists* (Gergen 1985). They are guilty of a major error, which tends to obscure their valuable theoretical contributions, and alienates many potentially sympathetic researchers. The theoretical causal-explanatory claim that many forms of human action and social practices are created and maintained (and in some cases eliminated) as a consequence of social discourse and negotiation has much to recommend it. Their metatheoretical or philosophical claim that many forms of human action and social practice are constituted by our social discourse about them has nothing to recommend it.

Social and scientific definition

It is not claimed that there is universal agreement with respect to the social definition of actions such as aggression, dishonesty, insults, and acts of suicide, although the amount of disagreement ought not to be exaggerated. The social psychological scientist may also feel disinclined to accept the definitions of laypersons, since they might not be best suited to a scientific analysis. However, neither of these points provide any good reason for denying the social relational and representational dimensions of human action. The mere fact of disagreements about the social definition of human actions and social practices between and among social psychological scientists and laypersons does not present any special problem, so long as the researcher provides a clear articulation of his or her own definition.

For example, experimental studies may suggest that 'violent stimuli'[3] tend to promote aggressive actions (Berkowitz and LePage 1967), defined by the experimenter as behaviours directed towards the injury of another, and discriminated in the experiments. Such an explanation may then be extended to cover everyday instances of aggression that satisfy this definition and that are preceded by exposure to violent stimuli. Such explanations cannot of course be presumed to apply to instances of aggression that satisfy a different definition, for example simply in terms of actual or probable harm to another (few would be likely to endorse this definition, for it would classify many medical interventions and accidental injuries as acts of aggression). However, whether it does or not can be determined in the usual way by experimental or other empirical studies designed to establish whether violent stimuli also promote these forms of aggression thus defined. The point of a clear articulation of a particular social definition of action in terms of constitutive social relations and representations is to facilitate communication, replication, and explanatory inference in social psychological science, not to ensure consensus or concordance with any privileged definition.

Nevertheless, the scientific researcher's definition of actions such as aggression and dishonesty cannot stray too radically from the social definitions of participants in a form of social life, if she wishes her empirically tested theories to provide explanations of those actions that most persons would describe as aggressive. Too many researchers suppose that epistemic objectivity is served by operational definitions of actions in terms of physical movements. This only serves the convenience of experimenters by making life easier for them. It does nothing to promote epistemic objectivity. On the contrary, it regularly undermines it.

Thus an experimentalist may operationally define aggression in terms of the physical movement of a switch on a shock generator (Milgram 1974), or an investigator may define dishonesty in terms of claims to ownership made by subjects who retrieve coins intentionally dropped close by them by experimental confederates in supermarkets (Farrington and Kidd 1977). Experimenters are of course free to define actions in any way they please. They cannot, however, maintain epistemic objectivity if they then go on to claim, as they invariably do, that empirically supported explanations of aggression and dishonesty – operationally defined – based upon such experiments and field studies can be generalized to cover real-life instances of aggression and dishonesty – defined in socially conventional ways in terms of social relations and representations.

If subjects in field studies of dishonesty, for example, mistakenly suppose that coins dropped close by them by experimenters are in fact their own, then we cannot suppose that explanations of their behaviour that are empirically based upon such studies throw any light upon the theoretical explanation of dishonest actions. For if this is the case, then the actions of experimental subjects are simply not dishonest according to the conventional social definition. It is in fact not unreasonable to suppose that many persons who hear coins dropping close by them would conclude that they had dropped coins of their own (only those few who knew they carried no coins would be likely to conclude otherwise), and that therefore their actions of retaining them and claiming that they were their own could not be described as dishonest.

Of course there are all kinds of methodological and epistemological problems concerning the determination of whether subjects in experimental and field studies represent their behaviours as directed towards the injury of others or the removal of goods that rightly belong to another. However, operational definitions of human actions do nothing to resolve these problems; they simply enable the researcher to ignore them.

The frequent exclusive focus on 'observable behaviour' as the object of social psychological science enables many researchers to simply abandon their responsibility for ensuring that the social relational and representational dimensions of human action are reproduced and discriminated in experimental and field studies. This casts serious doubt upon the explanatory relevance of such studies. The reason many researchers get away with it is because of a critical ambiguity of the term 'behaviour'. This may be taken in the first place to refer to observable physical movements. In this sense we talk about the behaviour of planets and of balls rolling down inclined planes, and it is of course in this sense that researchers frequently employ the term to characterize the outcomes of experimental and other empirical studies. The term 'behaviour' may also be taken to refer to those socially located and intentionally directed human behaviours that are constituted as human actions by their social relational and representational dimensions. In this sense we tell our children to behave themselves (in personally responsible and socially acceptable ways) and apologise for our own behaviour (that is socially unacceptable and irresponsible), and it in this sense that researchers employ the term when making explanatory inferences from experimental and other empirical studies to everyday human actions in the social world. Yet as the above considerations suggest, behaviours defined in the former fashion cannot be presumed to be equivalent to behaviours defined in the latter fashion. No physical movement in an experimental study can be identified as an aggressive action unless it is determined that it was directed towards the injury of another.

It is worth stressing again that the point of the present analysis is not to recommend any privileged or preferred definition of actions and social practices. It is rather to insist that socially meaningful actions such as aggression, dishonesty, and suicide are not constituted as actions by any physical dimensions common to any range of behaviours, or by any form of descriptive discourse about them. It is to insist that physically diverse forms of behaviour are constituted as forms of action by social relations and representations.

Again this ought to be obvious to anyone engaged in social life in the normal ways, never mind those engaged in the scientific study of it. It is nevertheless worth stressing just because so many researchers are disinclined to accept it, for no good reason. For it is precisely because many behaviours are as a matter of fact intentionally directed and socially located that we require an explanatory social psychological science: that is, a science concerned to furnish empirically-supported explanations of socially meaningful human actions and social practices. Anyone who denies this and recommends a 'pure' scientific analysis of behaviour in its place effectively abandons social psychological science, by simply identifying the explanatory domain of such a science with the explanatory domain of other sciences such as physics and biology.

Description and explanation

There are those who would dispute that it is a matter of fact that human actions are intentionally directed and socially located, who would claim that our descriptions of human actions in terms of social relations and representations embody a theoretical perspective upon human behaviour that could be, and arguably ought to be, abandoned (Churchland 1979).

However, this 'eliminativist' claim is based upon a fundamental error that is shared by a great many researchers. Many researchers seem reluctant to accept that human actions are constituted by their social relational and representational dimensions for the following reason. They believe that classificatory descriptions of actions based upon such dimensions are somehow 'theory-informed' in an objectionable way: that they somehow presuppose causal explanations of actions in terms of social relations and representations. In general it is supposed that to acknowledge the socially meaningful nature of human action is somehow to prejudge explanatory issues in favour of the conventional reasons avowed by participants in a form of social life.

This is perhaps understandable since many defenders of the socially meaningful nature of action do seem to imply this. However, this popular conception is quite mistaken. Classificatory descriptions of human actions in terms of social relations and representations are quite *neutral* with respect to explanatory questions. Thus, for example, a behaviour may be said to be an act of aggression if and only if it is directed by the agent towards the injury of another. Yet aggressive actions so constituted and defined may sometimes be best explained in terms of exposure to 'violent stimuli', and at other times may best be explained in terms of aggressive drives or planned revenge. If classificatory descriptions of actions did presuppose particular explanations of them, then it would be contradictory to advance alternative explanations of them. However, there is no contradiction involved in supposing that some instances of 'bystander apathy' (the intentional neglect of an injured person) are caused by failures of social perception (Latané and Darley 1970), but that some others are a product of social anxiety, and that others still are the product of the quite callous attitudes of some persons. Yet there would be if the classification of an action as apathetic presupposed any of these particular explanations.

An especially common error concerns the *intentionality* of most human actions. We have noted that many behaviours are constituted as human actions by agents' representations of the point and purpose of their behaviour. This suggests that descriptions of actions that ascribe such representational dimensions somehow provide special support for certain forms of psychological explanation of action, and in particular those forms of psychological explanation that are likely to be avowed by the agents themselves. Yet again this is just a mistake. The fact that many behaviours are constituted as actions by their purposive direction does not establish that such actions are best explained in terms of agents' purposes (avowed or not). Many aggressive actions constituted as such by their purposeful direction may be best explained in terms of hypothalamic excitations caused by diet or drink, demonstrating avowed reasons in terms of revenge to be inoperative rationalizations. Of course equally they may not. The point to be stressed is that these questions are properly empirical questions to be determined by empirical research, since no particular form of explanation is presupposed by descriptions of actions that attribute representational dimensions.

One of the reasons why we may be liable to be misled into confusing agent representations that are constitutive of human actions and agent reasons referenced in causal explanations that are not, is because on occasions agent representations do also function as causal explanatory reasons. Thus, for example, diverse behaviours are constituted as acts of helping by their being purposively directed by the agent to the relief of the distress of another. On occasions it may be true of some agents that they helped another for that reason alone: that is, they helped another for the sole reason of relieving their distress. On these occasions a reference to the agent's representation that constitutes her behaviour as an act of helping also provides the best theoretical explanation. These occasions are perhaps rarer than we would like to imagine.

On other occasions agents may help others for self-presentational reasons (to impress friends or colleagues) or in the hope of financial reward. Analogously an agent's representation of his behaviour as directed towards the injury of another constitutes his behaviour as an aggressive action. Sometimes his only reason for acting aggressively may be to bring about the injury of another (for its own sake, as it were). It is to be hoped that these occasions *are* as rare as we like to imagine. Again these are properly empirical questions to be determined by empirical research. They are not in any way predetermined or prejudged by the correct description of an action as an act of helping or aggression.

It is of course true that there is a respect in which descriptions of actions attributing agent representations may sometimes be said to presuppose a partial causal explanation. An agent's representation of his or her behaviour as directed towards the injury of another is a logically necessary condition of aggressive action, but it may also be conceived as a causally necessary condition. That is, it may be claimed that agents would not act aggressively unless they represented their action as directed towards the injury of another, that this is a temporally antecedent necessary condition for the generation of aggressive action.

Two points are worth stressing. The first is that even if such agent representations sometimes function as causally necessary conditions, such causally necessary conditions will be presupposed by all competing causal explanations in terms of causally sufficient conditions, and (as noted above) it is an empirical question whether such causally necessary conditions also function as causally sufficient conditions in any particular case. Thus competing explanations of aggression in terms of 'violent stimuli' or motives of revenge may both involve the presupposition that agent representations of intended injury are causally necessary conditions of aggressive actions, and it is an empirical matter in any particular case whether such representations also function as causally sufficient conditions (whether they function as causal-explanatory reasons for aggressive actions).

Second, not all agent representations that are logically necessary conditions of human actions can also be plausibly conceived as causally necessary conditions. My receipt and retention of a valuable item incorrectly mailed to me is a dishonest action if I recognize that the valuable item does not belong to me. However, it is not plausible to suppose that my representation of my behaviour as the receipt and retention of an item that rightly belongs to another is a causally necessary condition of my dishonest action, since the behaviour that I represent in this fashion temporally precedes my constitutive representation of it.

In sum, the correct description and identification of human actions constituted by social relational and representational dimensions does not presuppose the accuracy of any particular form of explanation of them. In particular the social relational dimensions of some actions do not imply that their best explanation is in terms of social relations, nor do the representational dimensions of other actions imply that their best explanation is in terms of agent's avowed purposes or reasons. Thus, for example, the decisions of jurors are partially constituted as decisions of jurors by their location within the social context of trial by jury, but the best explanation of their decisions may make reference to idiosyncrasies of their psychological biographies. Aggressive actions are constituted as aggressive actions by agent representations of their behaviour as directed towards the injury of another, but the best explanation of some acts of aggression may make reference to the social relations embedded in the institutional contexts of authoritarian structures (Milgram 1974).

All the points made in this chapter about the social constitution of actions in terms of social relations and representations are points about the *identity* of human actions that entail no causal explanatory commitments. Consequently suggestions that our 'folk-psychological' forms of descriptive classification of human actions in terms of social relations and representations ought to be, or are likely to be, rejected because of the possible or likely failure of our 'folk-psychological' causal explanations of them can be dismissed. Critics such as Churchland (1979) argue that since our forms of action classification are theoretical, then they ought to be rejected if the theories presupposed by them turn out to be false.

In one innocuous respect our system of action classification is of course theoretical: it is a system of linguistic descriptions that involve the attribution of (representational) properties and (social) relations to human behaviours, as opposed to other non-descriptive forms of linguistic expression such as commands or promises etc.[4] It is also theoretical in another familiar respect, insofar as it is often claimed that the properties and relations attributed by our action descriptions cannot be 'directly observed' in the fashion of tables and trees and physical movements. However, our system of action classification is not theoretical in another familiar and important respect: it does not presuppose any form of theoretical *causal explanation* of such actions, including those that may be classified as 'folk-psychological'. Consequently we would not be obliged to reject it or abandon it even if many or all of these theoretical causal explanations turned out to be demonstrably false (which may be seriously doubted).

Of course in order to maintain such a system we ought to have independent grounds for supposing that many behaviours do in fact have the social relational and representational dimensions we attribute to them. We do have such grounds. The contentful representations of behaviours that are referenced by our action descriptions are revealed in our everyday discourse about the likely consequences of human behaviours. Agents regularly articulate their knowledge of the likely harmful effects of certain behaviours, honestly avow that they are aiming to harm another, and engage in behaviours likely to cause harm to another. We have a wealth of evidence to support the claim that agents regularly act intentionally: that their behaviours are directed to the goals they regularly avow.

That is, our theoretical action descriptions are of course subject to empirical evaluation. They are confirmable and falsifiable. Their adequacy as theoretical descriptions does not however depend in any way upon the accuracy of 'folk-psychological' explanations of the forms of behaviour referenced by them. Consequently we would not be obliged or inclined to reject them even if most of our 'folk-psychological' explanations of the forms of behaviour referenced by them turned out to be false.

Natural and social psychological kinds

Although the recognition of the social relational and representational dimensions of human action does not pose any threat to objectivity or prejudge any explanatory questions, it does have a number of significant implications for social psychological science. For the above analysis suggests the very real possibility that there may be different *forms of action* in different cultures and historical periods. This possible ontological diversity is simply a consequence of the fact that human actions and social practices form *social psychological kinds* rather than *natural kinds*: they are constituted as forms of action and social practice by their social relational and representational dimensions rather than by their physical dimensions. Thus behaviours may be constituted as different forms of actions and practices in different cultures and historical periods by differences in social relations and representations. For example there are few polygamous marriages in the West or East and few instances of couvade (the practice whereby husbands simulate the birth pangs of their wives) outside of the Amazon. There are very few slaves these days and no longer any feudal duties. There can be no acts of dishonesty in societies that do not recognize property relations, and acts of ritual cannibalism (behaviours directed towards the ingestion of the mana of kings or enemies) can only occur in societies committed to some form of belief in the supernatural.

This possible diversity is not itself a product of different social descriptions, since such descriptions play no role in the constitution of actions and practices. Rather, differences in descriptions tend to be a product of differences in social relations and representations. It is always an objective question whether there are instances of aggression or feudal duties in other cultures, or instances of racism and dishonesty in our own, according to *any* social definition of these phenomena. Thus it is an objective question whether there are aggressive actions in our own or another culture according to a social definition of aggression in terms of behaviours directed towards the injury of others, or in terms of behaviours that cause or are likely to cause injury to another.

It is not a necessary condition of the presence of aggressive or dishonest actions in any culture that there are descriptions in that culture that translate into English as 'aggression' or 'dishonesty'.[5] It is only necessary that the language and conventions of that culture enable agents to represent their behaviours as directed towards the injury of others or to treat certain goods or services as rightly belonging to another. It is sufficient that some agents in that culture represent some of their behaviours in these terms.

The ontological items of the physical world studied by natural science are determined by the composition and structure of the physical world, not by our more or less useful definitions and descriptions of them. Precisely analogously the ontological items of the social psychological world are determined by social relations and representations, and not by our more or less useful definitions and descriptions of them. The significant difference is that whereas the constitutive compositional and structural dimensions of the physical world are well known to remain largely invariant across time and space, this cannot be presumed to be the case with respect to the social relational and representational dimensions of the social psychological world.

Of course it must be stressed that this is an empirical question, to be determined by historical and cross-cultural research. It should also be stressed that this question is quite independent of any similarities and differences in behaviour that may be found to exist. For identical forms of behaviour may be constituted as quite different forms of action in different cultures and historical periods. Thus, pointing to someone is a means of identification in most Western cultures, and a means of insulting someone in many Eastern ones. Conversely different forms of behaviour do not of necessity mark different forms of action. Persons can get married in a variety of different behavioural ways in different cultures, by taking vows, by drinking tea, by leaping through fires, by accepting gifts, and by urinating into tin pots (this last in the Western Hebrides).

Despite the real possibility of such ontological diversity, it equally cannot be assumed. We should be especially careful not to mistake differences in social definitions of actions and practices for real ontological diversity, for references to the same basic social relations and representations may be differentially combined in different social definitions. We must also be very careful not to mistake differences in symbolic conventions for real differences in social relations and representations, for the same fundamental social relations and representations may be multifariously expressed according to the local conventions of different cultures and historical periods. Thus reputations may be gained in some cultures and lost in others by sparing the enemy; religious rituals may be characterized by their extravagance in some historical periods and their frugality in others.

Now the possibility of ontological diversity in the social world often leads to familiar doubts about the *universality* of theoretical explanations in social psychological science (Gergen 1973). Such theoretical knowledge would appear to be rather rigidly bound to specific historical periods and cultures. For example our explanation of the actions of Aztec priests and Japanese geishas seem to have no obvious bearing upon our explanation of the actions of English civil servants. Now this may be the case with respect to some of our explanations of social psychological phenomena.

However, it demonstrates neither a lack of universality nor any form of inadequacy.

The universality of an explanation must be carefully distinguished from its generality, and both must be distinguished from the frequency of manifestation of the phenomenon explained. An explanation is *universal* if it applies to each and every instance of a re-identifiable phenomenon, no matter how frequent or rare is the actual manifestation of that phenomenon. Thus there may be universal explanations of plutonium sickness, the creation of solar systems, infanticide and couvade despite the rarity of the manifestation of such phenomena. An explanation is non-universal if there is a variety of explanations of instances of a re-identifiable phenomenon: thus the explanation of aggression is not universal if some instances of aggression are best explained in terms of precipitating 'violent stimuli', and others best explained in terms of motives of revenge or excitations of the lateral hypothalamus.

Although instances of some actions and practices such as ritual cannibalism and feudal duties may no longer be re-identifiable, because they may no longer exist, this poses no threat to the universality of their explanation. This is common enough in natural science. Explanations of the behaviour of dinosaurs or the medieval strain of the bubonic plague may be universal even though these phenomena no longer exist. The adequacy of any of these explanations is solely a function of the quality of the evidence in favour of them.

An explanation is *general* if it provides an explanation for a range of different phenomena, again irrespective of how frequently these phenomena are manifested. Thus an explanation of a particular disease by bacillus transmission is general if it also provides an explanation of other diseases, however rare or frequent they may be. An explanation may be general even though it is not universal. Thus a reference to the inhalation of tobacco smoke may provide an explanation of only some lung cancers (others may be caused by genetic factors), but may also provide an explanation of some instances of bronchitis and heart disease. Analogously, some explanations of human actions and practices may be general even though they are not universal. Thus a reference to social pressures on conformity may explain only some instances of 'destructive obedience' (Milgram 1974), but may also provide an explanation of some instances of racism and teenage pregnancies. A reference to motives of revenge may explain only some instances of aggression, but may also provide an explanation of some instances of dishonesty and suicide.

These examples may suggest that explanations of human actions are more likely to be general than universal. This may turn out to be the case. What needs to be stressed is that this is an empirical question. There is no good reason for supposing that such explanations cannot be universal: the outcomes of all marriages may best be explained in terms of negotiated power relations. Neither is there any good reason for supposing that such explanations cannot be universal and general: a reference to negotiated power relations may also provide the best explanation of some, many, or all human sacrificial rituals and employment interviews.

These are properly empirical matters to be determined by social psychological research. The point to be stressed is that the possible non-universality of our explanations of human action does not cast any doubt upon their adequacy, for the universality of an explanation is no measure of its adequacy. The adequacy of any form of explanation in any science is determined by its accuracy, and the only measure of its accuracy is the quality of the evidence in support of it. The *scope* of an explanation is an entirely separate question.

This is worth stressing because we cannot anticipate that our explanations of human action will turn out to be universal. This is simply a consequence of the fact that human actions and social practices form social psychological kinds rather than natural kinds. Behaviours are constituted as actions by their social relational and representational dimensions rather than their physical dimensions. We have the logical right to presume that our explanations of the properties and behaviour of physical objects will be universal precisely because physical objects are constituted and defined in terms of those intrinsic compositional and structural dimensions that centuries of scientific experience has taught us play an important role in the explanation of their properties and behaviour. Thus we always give the same explanation of the corrosive power of acids or the conductive properties of metals in terms of their composition and structure.

We have no such right to presume the same with respect to human actions. The social relational and representational dimensions that enable some agents to dominate or imprison others, or which promote honesty or dishonesty or altruism or egoism may be quite different in different historical periods and cultures. The reasons for and causes of medieval aggression and suicide may be entirely different from the reasons for and causes of contemporary Western aggression and suicide, which may in turn be quite different from Far Eastern reasons for and causes of the *same forms of action*. We cannot presume that explanations will universally apply to each and every instance of an action re-identifiable in terms of social relations and representations. This is because such constitutive social relations and representations *may not* play any role in the causal explanation of such actions.

This is not to deny that they might. It is simply to note that the ontology of human action carries no presumptions about the universality of explanations. Thus we should not be surprised if we discover that our explanations do not universally apply, or assume that there is something wrong with our social psychological science if this proves to be the case. It may very well just be a brute fact about the social psychological world that different instances of forms of action such as aggression, dishonesty, and suicide must be explained in different ways in our own and other cultures.

There are those who have argued that social psychological 'sciences' cannot be scientific, precisely because human actions do not form natural kinds that can figure in universal laws (Rosenberg 1980; Wilkes 1984). However there seems to be good reason for requiring that the universality of explanations be treated as a criterion of scientific respectability. This appears to be merely a contingent feature of some explanations of some phenomena in some sciences. It cannot be treated as a criterion for the adequacy of any form of science, for if in fact all phenomena do have universal explanations, this is a fact about the world that can only be determined by scientific research. It is not a fact that is vouchsafed by any prescriptive definition of science. And it may very well not be a fact about the world.

Some might be tempted to suppose that we ought to resolve this perceived problem by operationally defining actions in terms of 'observable physical movements' and/or their effects, or by ignoring human actions completely and simply focusing on 'observable physical movements'. As suggested earlier, this would be to abandon social psychological science. Furthermore, if there is a problem, it will not be resolved by this expedient. There may be a variety of reasons for and causes of aggressive actions defined in terms of behaviours directed towards the injury of others. There are likely to be many more reasons for, and causes of, aggressive actions defined in terms of behaviours that cause or are likely to cause the injury of others. These will include all the reasons for and causes of many actions normally considered to be aggressive (namely those that are successfully directed towards the injury of others), *plus* all the reasons for, and causes of, surgical interventions that do more harm than good and accidental injuries. Or consider the myriad possible reasons for, and causes of, 'observable physical movements' such as 'arm-raising': these will include all the possible reasons for, and causes of, auction-bids, aggression, hailing a taxi, and saluting the Fuehrer.

Even if the classification of human actions in terms of physical movements and/or their effects promoted the discovery of universal explanations, this would not provide us with a compelling reason for abandoning our system of classification of human actions in terms of social relations and representations. In the natural sciences, we have no vested moral interest in classifying entities in terms of one set of dimensions rather than another. So we happily abandon or ignore systems of classification of physical entities in terms of their colour or smell in favour of a system of classification in terms of their physical composition and structure, which does promote successful universal explanations of their properties.

The situation is notably different in social psychological science. For in this case we do have a vested moral interest in a system of classification of actions in terms of social relations and representations. For it is precisely those forms of action such as aggression, dishonesty, helping, suicide, etc. that are proper objects of our moral concern as well as our intellectual interest. As noted above, the lack of universality of an explanation is not any indicator of its inadequacy. If the classification of actions in terms of their social psychological dimensions means we have to abandon presumptions or hopes about the universality of explanations in order to maintain their relevance to our moral and social concerns, then it seems a small price to pay. Especially since they might still turn out to be universal.[6]

2

SOCIAL DIMENSIONS OF MIND

Many of the points made in the previous chapter about human action may be generalized to human psychology. Much of human psychology may be said to be socially constituted in the following respect: many emotions and motives are constituted as emotions and motives by socially learned and negotiated forms of representation and evaluation of actions and social relations. Thus, for example, the emotion of shame is constituted as the emotion of shame by the representation of an action (or failure to act) as personally degrading and humiliating. The motive of revenge is constituted as the motive of revenge by the representation of an action as restitution for a prior injury.[1] The socially meaningful contents of many emotions and motives are appropriated from the socially meaningful contents of linguistic descriptions and evaluations, as are the socially meaningful contents of our beliefs, theories, and other psychological states.[2]

Although our classificatory descriptions of our psychological states are also socially learned and negotiated, they play no role in the constitution of them. Our classificatory descriptions of psychological phenomena as instances of shame or motive of revenge are linguistically objective: they are true or false according to whether the phenomena concerned have the properties attributed to them by our descriptions. Thus a psychological state may be accurately described as shame if and only if it involves the representation of an action (or failure to act) as personally degrading and humiliating; a psychological state may be accurately described as a motive of revenge if and only if it involves the representation of an action as restitution for a prior injury. It is neither a necessary nor a sufficient condition of shame or motive of revenge that it is described or represented by the agent or any observer as 'shame' or 'motive of revenge'. It is necessary and sufficient that it involves the representation of an action (or failure to act) as personally degrading and humiliating or as restitution for a prior injury (that it has the properties referenced by our descriptions 'shame' and 'motive of revenge').

The social dimensions of psychological states are not a logical consequence of the social dimensions of our descriptions of them. It is not necessary for a person to be ashamed that he or any other observer describes or represents his emotion as 'shame'. Children have to learn to be ashamed, to treat certain actions (or failure to act) as personally degrading and humiliating, before they come to learn the usage of the linguistic description 'shame'. They can be ashamed even if they do not recognize that their emotion is described as 'shame' in their form of social life. Analogously, many Americans may experience angst without recognizing that this emotion is described as 'angst' in another form of social life.

Psychological states are not constituted in any way or to any degree *as psychological states* by our descriptions or linguistically informed representations of them as instances of psychological states such as 'shame' or 'motive of revenge'. Our classificatory descriptions of such psychological states are descriptions of states that may be said to be *preformed* as psychological states by their socially meaningful contents and intentional direction. Thus my anger with my wife is constituted as anger with my wife by my representation of her actions as an offence against my dignity, and not by my description (or representation informed by a description) of my psychological state. The representations that are constitutive of shame and motive of revenge are directed upon actions and not upon these psychological states themselves.[3] In general, the representational states that are constitutive of psychological states are directed upon aspects of reality *other* than the psychological states themselves.

The Schachter–Singer experiment

Much confusion about these matters has been engendered by a common and very popular misconception of the implications of the Schachter–Singer experiment (1962), which is frequently held to have demonstrated that emotions are constituted by 'social labelling', by our descriptions or linguistically informed representations of them as particular emotional states. It did not demonstrate any such thing.

In this experiment subjects were asked to take part in an experiment to test the effects of a new drug ('suproxin') on vision. They were actually given injections of norepinephrine which stimulated sympathetic arousal. They were then asked to wait in a room until the drug took effect, in the company of another 'subject' who was in fact an experimental confederate. Those subjects who were unaware of the cause of their sympathetic arousal (they were uninformed or misinformed about the actual effects of the injection) labelled their arousal states in accord with the social cues provided by the confederates in the two experimental conditions. In the 'anger' condition the confederate reacted with anger to a questionnaire provided by the experimenter; most subjects in this condition described their emotional state as 'anger'. In the 'euphoria' condition the confederate acted in a jolly and carefree manner, making paper planes and cavorting with a hula-hoop; most subjects in this condition described their emotional state as 'euphoria'.

The results of this experiment are consistent with the experimental hypothesis that in such ambiguous situations our descriptions of our emotional states are influenced by social cues, and not based upon any perceived physiological differences between anger and euphoria (contra the called 'James–Lange' theory which suggests that they are). The experiment does not demonstrate anything about the constitution of emotion itself.

Schachter later claimed (1965) that most emotions are physiologically homogeneous, that diverse emotions are not constituted as diverse emotions by physiologically diverse arousal states. He suggested that homogeneous arousal states are constituted as diverse emotional states by cognitive labelling based upon social cues: my homogeneous arousal states are constituted as anger when I label them as 'anger', and are constituted as 'euphoria' when I label them as 'euphoric', etc. However, this claim is certainly not demonstrated by the Schachter–Singer experiment.

The behaviour of subjects in this experiment can be readily explained in linguistically objective terms: subjects in the 'anger' and 'euphoria' conditions were genuinely angry and euphoric and consequently correctly described their emotional states as 'anger' and 'euphoria'. Subjects in the 'anger' condition may have treated the questionnaire as genuinely offensive: it did in fact include intrusive questions about their parents' sexual and ablutive habits (wouldn't you be angry?). Subjects in the 'euphoria' condition may have enjoyed the jolly company (don't you sometimes?).

Citing the Schachter–Singer experiment, Heelas (1981: 13) echoes many commentators in suggesting that: 'recent theorizing in the psychology of emotions suggests that emotional experiences are in fact constituted by conceptual systems'. However, the Schachter–Singer experiment does nothing to suggest that emotional experiences are constituted by the employment of concepts expressed by our descriptions of our emotional states (as instances of 'anger', 'euphoria', 'shame', etc.). It is entirely consistent with a linguistically objective account of emotion descriptions that treats emotions as independently constituted by representational contents. According to this account, the only concepts that are constitutive of emotions are those informing the socially meaningful contents of representations of actions and social relations that are constitutive of emotions.

Too many writers also rush to the conclusion that emotions must be constituted by emotional labelling, since emotions do not appear to be independently constituted by diverse physiological states.[4] Of course this simply does not follow. According to a linguistically objective account of emotion descriptions, emotions are independently constituted by diverse forms of representations of actions and social relations. Furthermore this line of reasoning does not easily generalize to psychological phenomena such as motives or beliefs, descriptions of which are plainly not employed to characterize states of arousal that might turn out to be homogeneous.

Intensional contents and intentional objects

The identity of psychological states such as belief, emotion, and motivation is determined by their *intensional contents* – the socially meaningful contents of representations appropriated from the socially meaningful contents of language – and their *intentional objects* – the objects to which our psychological states are directed. Thus an agent's belief *that the Eiffel Tower is in Paris* is constituted as that particular belief by the fact that she represents the Eiffel Tower [the intentional object of her belief] as being in Paris [the intensional content of her belief]. An agent's shame is constituted as that particular emotion by the fact that he represents a particular action of his such as cheating [the intentional object of his emotion] as personally degrading and humiliating [the intensional content of his emotion]. We may thus express our earlier point about the non-constitutive role of descriptions of psychological states by noting that such psychological states never reflexively take themselves as intentional objects.

This characterization of the identity of psychological states carries no causal explanatory implications. A common and fair complaint about the early versions of the American Psychiatric Association's *Diagnostic and Statistical Manual of Mental Disorders* (DSM) was that many of its classificatory descriptions presupposed particular psychoanalytic explanations. However, later versions such as DSM-III (APA 1980) appear to have gone too far in their attempt to be theoretically noncommittal, by not requiring any representational dimensions for disorders such as depression.[5] Yet it is a mistake to suppose that the recognition of the representational dimensions of depression prejudges any casual-explanatory issues. A definition of depression in terms of representations of hopelessness or helplessness, for example, would not entail any causal-explanatory account of depression. Some instances of depression may be best explained in psychoanalytic terms, and other instances may best be explained in terms of classical or operant conditioning. In particular, it would not entail any psychological explanation of depression. It is entirely consistent with the possibility that all instances of depression are biological in origin. It is also entirely consistent with the supposition that some instances of depression are biological in origin, some psychological in origin, and others social in origin.

Once again a number of qualifications are in order to avoid misinterpretation. To claim that psychological states such as emotions and motives are constituted as emotions and motives by contentful representational states is not to claim (or suggest) that psychological states such as emotions and motives (or beliefs, for that matter) are 'images' or 'copies' or 'reflections' of the reality represented. The term 'representation' is employed merely to indicate the contentful and directed nature of such psychological states.

To claim that psychological states such as emotions and motives are constituted as emotions and motives by agent representations of actions and social relations is not to claim that it is a necessary condition of these psychological states that the agent is conscious of or can articulate the content of such states. Thus agents may *misdescribe* their emotions and motives, despite the constitutive role of such representations. The degree to which agents can have access to the contents of their psychological states is an important epistemological issue, which will be discussed in Chapter 6. However, it must be stressed again that this epistemological issue is logically independent of the issue concerning linguistic objectivity. The linguistic objectivity of our descriptions of psychological states can be maintained even if we come to accept that it is enormously difficult (or even impossible in principle) to determine their truth or falsity with any reasonable degree of assurance.

Constatives and performatives

Social constructionists frequently base their denials of linguistic objectivity upon denials of epistemic objectivity. However, their denials of the linguistic objectivity of psychological discourse are sometimes based on independent grounds. They sometimes claim that our psychological discourse – our discourse putatively about psychological states – is simply not descriptive.

It is frequently claimed that psychological discourse is *performative* (Gergen 1989: 71; Shotter 1989: 3): it is employed to perform social functions other than description, such as warning, excusing, endorsing, etc. According to this account, avowals of depression, for example, are employed to excuse one's behaviour rather than to describe one's psychological state.

This distinction between descriptions and performatives is based upon J.L. Austin's (1962) distinction between *constative* and *performative* utterances, between utterances that are *sayings* such as descriptions, and utterances that are *doings* such as warnings and promises. Constative utterances such as 'The cat is on the mat' or 'Elements are composed of atoms' are putative descriptions of independent states of affairs, and may be properly characterized as true or false. Performative utterances such as 'I promise to repay you the money tomorrow' and 'I apologise for forgetting your birthday' perform the social functions of promising and apologizing. They are not putative descriptions of independent states of affairs, and cannot be characterized as true or false, although they may be characterized as effective or ineffective, sincere or insincere, etc. Social constructionists claim that psychological discourse is performative and not constative.

However, Austin himself quickly realized that the distinction between constatives and performatives is not mutually exclusive, and eventually admitted that constatives are simply one kind of performative that serves the social function of description. He argued that his earlier distinction should be abandoned in favour of the recognition that different forms of *speech acts* such as describing, warning, promising, etc. can serve a variety of social and communicative functions. On this account, the same social or communicative function can be served by a variety of linguistic utterances. Thus I can perform the speech act of warning by employing a 'performative' or non-descriptive utterance such as 'Beware the Ides of March' or a 'constative' or descriptive utterance such as 'You will be assassinated on the Ides of March'.

The point is that speech acts can be descriptive *and* performative. The undoubted fact that psychological discourse can be employed to perform all sorts of social functions such as excusing, warning, etc. does not demonstrate or even suggest that it cannot also be employed to perform a descriptive function. These functions are simply not exclusive. There is no reason at all to suppose, for example, that depression avowals cannot be employed both to excuse our behaviour *and* to describe our unfortunate psychological state. Indeed the descriptive function of depression avowals provides the most natural explanation of their social power to excuse.

To affirm the linguistic objectivity of psychological descriptions is not to deny or underestimate the degree of social construction and linguistic negotiation involved in the creation and maintenance (and elimination) of characteristically human emotions and motives. On the contrary, it is recognized that most forms of emotion and motive are derived from our socially negotiated linguistic commentaries upon our actions and social relations. Diverse emotions and motives in diverse forms of social life are largely a product of the diverse forms of linguistic commentaries upon actions and social relations to be found in diverse forms of social life. They are maintained by such forms of linguistic commentary upon actions and social relations, and cease to exist when such forms of linguistic commentary are no longer employed. To acknowledge this is, however, only to acknowledge the creative role of discourse about actions and social relations, not the constitutive role of discourse about emotions and motives.

Ontological diversity

Psychological states such as emotions, motives, and beliefs may also be said to form social psychological rather than natural kinds. They are constituted as psychological states by the socially meaningful contents of representational states directed upon intentional objects. As in the case of human actions, we can anticipate ontological diversity with respect to psychological states in different cultures and historical periods. This is patently obvious in the case of beliefs. It is clear that agents in different ages and different cultures hold different beliefs about the shape of the earth, the origins of disease, and the possibility of witchcraft. However, it also seems to be equally likely with respect to psychological phenomena such as emotion and motivation.

We do indeed discriminate differences in psychologies cross-culturally and transhistorically with respect to differences in intentional objects and intensional contents of local forms of social representation. In terms of differences with respect to intentional objects, we may note that the English take pride in their homes while Italians take pride in their sister's virginity. In sexually promiscuous ages and cultures persons may be envious of the castles and cattle of others but not of their husbands and wives.

More interesting perhaps are more fundamental differences with respect to socially meaningful intensional contents. Japanese 'amae' appears to be quite different from Western 'love' because it involves a 'fawning' dependency that contrasts starkly with Western notions of reciprocal support (Morsbach and Tyler 1976), although both are directed upon the same intentional objects (spouses, mistresses, friends). The early medieval emotion of 'accidie' involving a form of disgusted boredom with the world (Altschule 1965) appears quite different from the dark visions of 'the skull beneath the skin' characteristic of the Jacobean emotion of 'melancholie'. These in turn appear to be quite different from the representations of hopelessness and loss characteristic of much contemporary depression (Abramson, Metalsky, and Alloy 1989).

It should be similarly stressed (as in the case of action) that the degree of such ontological diversity is an entirely open question, to be determined by appropriate forms of empirical research. Furthermore it may be the case that there is a set of basic representational dimensions that can be re-identified in all ages and cultures, but which are differentially combined in such ages and cultures and characterized according to different social definitions. This is in fact suggested by Kemper's (1978) analysis of emotions in terms of representations of the status and power relations between self and others, which generates combinations of recognizable emotions for which there are no conventional classificatory descriptions, or only a loose collection of approximate descriptions in different languages. Again it must be stressed that this is an empirical question. We cannot presume that there are such universal basic dimensions, and should not be surprised or doubtful of the adequacy of our science if we do not discover any.

It should also be stressed again that whatever diversity there is is a product of differential social forms of representation of actions, and *not* the product of differential social forms of representation of psychological states themselves. Thus accidie for example was not created or constructed by representations *of* accidie, or by the employment of the classificatory description 'accidie'. Rather it was constituted by a form of representation of actions originally characteristic of monks in the sixth century, involving a disinclination to apply oneself to noonday prayers (for this reason it was often referred to as the 'noonday demon'). There is also some evidence that accidie may be re-identifiable in contemporary times, despite the fact that virtually no one who suffers from it would describe it as 'accidie' (or represent it in this linguistically informed fashion). The psychiatrist Robert Findley-Jones (1987) suggests that the General Health Questionnaire and the Present State Examination (two standard clinical tests) can be employed to discriminate accidie from contemporary forms of depression, and also that accidie appears at present to be particularly prevalent among housewives and the unemployed.

Psychology and language

Many researchers seem to confuse the role played by language in providing the socially meaningful contents of representations that are constitutive of emotions and motives with the role played by language in providing descriptions of emotions and motives thus constituted. Lewis and Saarni (1985: 8), for example, claim that 'emotional experience ... requires that organisms possess a language of emotion'. However, this claim is ambiguous. Emotions require a language of emotion only in the sense that they require a language that articulates the distinctions of the moral orders of the social world: that marks certain actions and social relations as degrading, insulting, honourable, achievements, failures, etc. The socially meaningful contents of our emotions are generally appropriated from such forms of moral commentary upon social actions, so that we come to represent certain actions as degrading, insulting, honourable, achievements, failures, etc. However, emotions do not require a language descriptive of emotion itself: a language comprising of descriptions such as 'anger', 'shame', 'accidie', etc.

This is simply a consequence of the linguistic objectivity of psychological descriptions. Acids and carbon would still exist even if we did not employ the descriptions 'acid' and 'carbon': there would still be solutions and elements that have the properties ascribed by our descriptions 'acid' and 'carbon'. Anger and motives of revenge could still exist even if we did not employ the descriptions 'anger' and 'motive of revenge': there could still be representational states having the properties ascribed by our descriptions 'anger' and 'motive of revenge'.

There would be no loss to our psychological lives if our language did not contain descriptions of our psychological states. Some cultures seem to have little social interest in reflecting upon their psychological states. As Hallpike (1979: 392) notes: 'the realm of purely private experience and motives, as distinct from the evaluation of actual behaviour, is given little attention in many primitive societies'. Some cultures, such as the Pintupi Aborigines of Western Australia (Myers 1979) and the Ommura of Papua New Guinea (Hallpike 1979) in fact have few descriptive terms for emotions and motives. It does not follow, nor is there evidence to suggest that it is the case, that the psychological lives of persons in such cultures are impoverished. The Taiwanese language has approximately 750 descriptions of emotion (Boucher 1979) and English only about 400 (Davitz 1969). It does not follow that the Taiwanese lead richer emotional lives than the English, and this is less than obviously the case. It would be hard to argue that the range and richness of emotions expressed in Taiwanese literature greatly exceeds the range and richness of emotions expressed in English literature. The range and richness of emotional life in any culture is a function of the range and richness of the language of moral commentary upon actions from which the contents of emotions are appropriated, and not a function of the number of linguistic terms that may be employed to describe emotions.

THE SOCIAL CONSTITUTION OF PERSONS

It might be objected that the above analysis simply begs important questions about the cognitive nature of emotions, and ignores associated neurological and physiological factors. However, this would be to confuse a question about the identity of emotion and other psychological states with a question concerning their physical incarnation, and the causal role that their form of physical incarnation plays in the generation or impediment of human action. For it appears that certain forms of representation are both necessary and sufficient for the presence of many emotions, for example. We cannot attribute shame to animals or rocks if we believe that such entities do not represent their behaviours as degrading and humiliating. Conversely, although neurophysiological factors do often have explanatory relevance with respect to those actions explained by reference to our emotional state, there is nothing logically paradoxical about attributing pride or shame to beings that are not physiologically aroused, or when they are not physiologically aroused. Despite perhaps dramatic differences in their physical composition, we would attribute anger and shame to Martians if we came to believe that they represented some of their actions in what we consider to be socially appropriate ways. Similarly there is nothing paradoxical about 'cold' or 'calm' anger and joy. Although perhaps rare at present, it may become common in a future age when we have learned to control our arousal via biofeedback techniques. Such emotions may still promote the appropriate forms of action. I may coldly refuse your request for additional funds because I am angry at your squandering of previous financial support. The calm but emotional performance of Sydney Carton on the guillotine is perhaps a fictional ideal, but it is not a logically incoherent one. The supposition that there are constitutive neurophysiological elements in the case of motives and other contentful psychological states such as beliefs is even less plausible, since we ascribe such psychological states in complete ignorance of their neurophysiological incarnation.[6]

This complaint is also something of a red herring, because although it seems clear that characteristically human emotions such as shame, guilt, disappointment, anger, envy, etc. form social psychological rather than natural kinds – they are constituted as particular forms of emotion by their socially meaningful contents rather than by their physical composition – it seems equally clear that emotion itself does not form any kind of thing at all (natural or social psychological). The types of phenomena that laypersons and psychologists characterize as emotions range from the startle reflex all the way through to the most notable sentiments of humankind. It is extremely doubtful that we could delineate any feature or set of features that could be convincingly described as necessary and sufficient conditions of emotion. Thus disputes between non-cognitive (Zajonc 1984) and cognitive theorists (Lazarus 1984) of emotion tend to degenerate into purely semantic disputes.

Personal identity

Nevertheless the above analysis is limited in the following respect. So far, psychological states have been characterized as social only insofar as their intensional contents have been characterized as socially meaningful and often directed upon social objects. While this limited account is sufficient to suggest the cross-cultural and transhistorical diversity of emotions and motives, and to defend the linguistic objectivity of our classificatory descriptions of such states, this is not the whole social story.

The point may be expressed in the following way with respect to emotion. It is obviously not sufficient for an emotion such as shame that an agent merely represents his action as the kind of action that is conventionally represented by social agents as degrading and humiliating. Rather he has to *treat* it as a personal degradation and humiliation. He must be concerned with the way in which it reflects upon his personal honour and dignity, with the way in which it reflects upon his *personal identity*. A person is only ashamed if he represents his action (or failure to act) as reflecting negatively upon his 'identity project' (Harré 1983): the goals and commitments that constitute the type of person he aims to be.

It may be said that our commitment to identity projects and our success and failure in executing them in the social world is constitutive of our personal identities. Such identity projects are best explicated in terms of commitment to (usually) a variety of moral careers (Goffman 1961): the culturally available routes for the creation and maintenance (and destruction) of public reputation and personal dignity within social collectives. Our identities are determined by our commitments to such identity projects and by our success (or failure) in meeting the social hazards and threats to our reputation and dignity that occur within social collectives.

These identity projects and the moral careers they encompass may also be said to be socially constituted in the following respect: they are forms of engagement in the social world governed by conventions of success and failure within social collectives. Identity projects are social and relational in nature and depend upon the types of social collectives and conventions indigenous to any culture or historical period. Thus we can longer pursue the identity projects and moral careers of feudal barons or samurai, nor can Westerners pursue the moral careers of witchdoctor or harem master.

Modern social psychological theories of identity tend to conceive of identity in terms of social labelling by self and others: one's identity is said to be determined by the linguistic descriptions applied to the agent by self and others, such as 'psychologist', 'politician', 'housewife', 'black', 'homosexual', etc. (Breakwell 1983). However, it is hard to understand just what is supposed to be determined by the application of these linguistically objective descriptions: one does not become a psychologist or homosexual by being described or represented as one by self or others. There are times when I like to think of myself as a psychologist (when, for example, I am critical of the neglect of psychological evidence by philosophers or when I get invited to address the APA) – but this does not make me one. I simply lack the social credentials.

Of course this is not to deny that linguistic discourse may play an enormously potent causal role in influencing my choice of identity project, or my success or failure within certain moral careers. The social ostracism I may face by being incorrectly characterized as 'homosexual' (perhaps by virtue of my physique or the pitch of my voice) may force me into the company of homosexuals, and through their influence I may become one. Entry into, and success or failure within many moral careers is powerfully influenced by the social labelling of individuals as 'female', 'black', 'homosexual', 'atheist', etc. (whether or not such descriptions are accurate or inaccurate). In many places and times, entry into some forms of moral career is simply closed to persons labelled according to sex, race, class, or religious affiliation, and success into many forms of moral career is impeded or advanced by such social labelling. These forms of discourse are enormously influential and thus a proper object of theoretical interest in the study of personal identity. Such discourse is, however, simply not constitutive of our identity.

The significance of this for emotion and motivation is as follows. The representational contents of most characteristically human emotions and motives may be said to be socially constituted in two further important respects. It is not only that their contents are socially meaningful appropriations of the contents of our moral commentary on actions. It is also the case that their contents are based upon the conventions of the local moral orders of specific forms of social collectives in which moral careers are pursued, and involve social engagement within such collectives. The forms of achievement and failure that may be seen as objects of pride and shame are based upon the diverse social conventions of the moral orders of diverse forms of social collective. The high grades that are a source of great pride to the committed academic student may be a source of embarrassment and shame to the gang leader. Commitment to the conventions of a social collective through social engagement is a condition of such emotions. I will not be embarrassed by my failure to establish my reputation as a skilful goalkeeper or ashamed of my unskilled performance in a charity match with another department of philosophy. The professional soccer player who trains as a goalkeeper would be.

The psychologies of persons

These respects in which emotions and motives may be said to be socially constituted are important to stress for the following reason. It cannot be assumed that social psychological scientists will discover law-like connections between particular psychological states and actions, when such states are defined in terms of intensional contents and intentional objects. And, intuitively, this seems most unlikely. For we do not suppose that there is a unique form of action or small finite set of actions produced by shame, for example. Rather what particular actions agents who are ashamed produce is determined by the role this form of representation plays within their perhaps quite different identity projects. Thus for some agents in some ages and cultures shame may provide a reason for altruistic action; for some agents in other ages and cultures it may provide a reason for suicide. For some agents in some social contexts disappointment may provide a reason for renewed and redirected effort; for other agents in different social contexts it may provide a reason for aggression or dishonesty.

Yet again it must be stressed that this is an empirical question. The point is again that we should not be surprised if we do not find law-like regularities between particular emotions or motives and particular actions, and should not treat our ability to discover them as some sort of measure of the adequacy of our explanations or our science. Once again this is simply a consequence of the fact that psychological phenomena form social psychological kinds. Their mode of ontological constitution does not have any implications about their causal directionality, and indeed any emotion, for example, may promote any form of action in any individual, given an appropriate background of social context and biography. Thus anger at a broken promise may promote aggressive actions, dishonest actions, acts of obedience, and disobedience, marriages and suicide, given different social contexts and psychological history.

The fundamental point to be made is that the theoretical identities of psychological states are relational in nature. Our psychologies are not mere aggregates of psychological atoms of belief, emotion, and motivation that could in principle exist independently of their relation to other psychological phenomena. They are, rather, necessarily integrated aspects of the world views and identity projects of human agents. The nature of our beliefs is determined by their position within whole networks of beliefs. Thus I cannot believe that the Empire State Building is the tallest building in the world without also believing a whole range of other things about the Empire State Building and tall structures that fix the reference and meaning of my belief (such as that the Empire State Building is in New York, that tall structures stand higher than low structures, etc.). The very nature of our emotions and motivations is determined by positions they occupy within our ongoing identity projects. They only have significance by virtue of our representations of the success or failure of our projected personal passages in the social world.

One claim only implicit in the above discussion is worth making explicit: persons are themselves social and relational in nature. Commitment to socially located identity projects may be treated as a necessary condition of personhood, insofar as the bulk of characteristically human emotions seem to be logically tied to the forms of moral commentary and conventions of social collectives. Charles Taylor (1977) has claimed that the capacity to form 'strong evaluations' – representations of the intrinsic worth of actions – is a necessary condition of personhood. These 'strong evaluations' can be readily identified with the socially diverse forms of commitment to identity projects within social collectives and the socially diverse forms of emotion and motivation encompassed by them.

Explanatory kinds

This suggests a final reason for rejecting complaints about social psychological science based upon the claim that the objects in its domain do not form natural kinds, and therefore cannot figure in universal laws. In the last chapter it was argued that it is unreasonable to treat the universality of an explanation as a measure of its explanatory adequacy. This is to illegitimately treat a contingent feature of some explanations in some scientific domains as a prescriptive requirement of an adequate scientific explanation. It is also worth noting that it is inappropriate to contrast human actions and psychological states that are not obviously governed by universal laws with physical entities such as acids and carbon that do seem to be regularly governed by universal laws. It is much more appropriate to compare the *behaviour and properties* of physical entities with human actions and psychological states. When we do this of course it is much less obvious that explanations of physical phenomena are always universal. In fact it is obviously the case that they are not. Some physical motions, such as the orbits of planets, can be explained in terms of gravitational forces. Other physical motions, such as the movement of a pin towards a magnet, and the orbit of an electron, are to be explained in terms of electromagnetic and weak nuclear forces.

The critical question is not whether entities form natural or social psychological kinds. The critical question is whether entities form *explanatory kinds*: whether a reference to their constitutive dimensions furnishes an adequate explanation of many of their properties and behaviours. References to the composition and structure of physical entities such as acids and carbon (the constitutive dimensions of such phenomena) are well known to furnish adequate explanations of their properties and behaviour. There would seem to be no good reason in principle for supposing that a reference to socially located identity projects (a constitutive dimension of personhood) cannot furnish an adequate explanation of many human actions and psychological states.[7]

In fact if there is any candidate for a universal causal explanatory principle of social psychological life, this is perhaps the best, at least on a certain upper level of abstraction. It may well be the case that the form of all distinctly human life is determined by such socially located identity projects, while the substance of individual lives may vary greatly with the cross-cultural and transhistorical diversity of forms of social collectivity, and the particularities and idiosyncrasies of individual biographies.

3

CAUSAL EXPLANATION

CAUSALITY AND CORRELATION

The avowed goal of social psychological science is to advance empirically-supported causal explanations of actions such as aggression, dishonesty, obedience, altruism, suicide, etc. But what is it to provide a causal explanation of an event or human action? Most social psychological scientists have come to accept some version of the 'regularity' account of causality, based upon the original analysis of the empiricist philosopher David Hume (1739).

The regularity account of causality

According to Hume, we have no knowledge of 'causal power' or 'force' or 'generation', because we have no sense experience of such phenomena. We normally think that in a causal sequence, such as the motion of one billiard ball causing motion in another, that there is some form of 'necessary connection' between the events. We feel that the motion of the first ball 'generates' or 'produces' the motion of the second, and that given the motion of the first ball, the second *must* move. But Hume denied the legitimacy of such suppositions. All we can observe in a causal sequence is the spacial and temporal contiguity (togetherness) of the events, the fact that the cause always precedes the effect, and that the events are 'constantly conjoined' in our experience. Since this is all we observe, this is all we can know about causality. There is no 'power' or 'necessary connection' that can be discriminated in the world. The only 'connection' is a psychological connection or association we make between events that are 'constantly conjoined' in our experience, and which we then (illegitimately) project upon the events themselves.

The essentials of this account were adopted by later generations of empiricists, positivists, and scientific empiricists. According to the 'regularity' account of causality (Braithwaite 1953; Hempel 1965), causal propositions or laws are held to refer to the constant conjunction or regular association between physical objects and events. The modification of this doctrine to include 'regular association' was designed to include causal explanations and laws in biological and social psychological sciences based upon statistical regularities rather than strict empirical invariance. Thus for example a causal explanation of aggressive actions by reference to the antecedent presence of 'violent stimuli' only makes reference to an established statistical correlation between violent stimuli and aggressive actions (Bell and Staines 1981).

According to this account, causal propositions are held to be confirmed by observations of 'positive instances' of the correlations they describe (Nagel 1939), and the degree of confirmation or probability of such causal propositions is held to be proportional to the number of observed 'positive' instances of the correlation (Carnap 1966).

Deductive–nomological explanation

This difference is also reflected in the standard scientific empiricist account of causal explanation (Hempel and Oppenheim 1948). According to this account, called the *deductive–nomological* account of scientific explanation, individual events are explained by the logical deduction of a description of these events from at least one 'covering law' and statement of 'initial conditions'. Thus, for example, the expansion of a gas is explained by the logical deduction of a description of the event – 'the gas expanded' – from a causal law covering this event – 'all heated gases expand' – and a statement of initial conditions – 'the gas was heated'. The event to be explained is called the 'explanandum' and the laws and initial conditions that do the explaining are called the 'explanans'. The 'covering law' is held to be a generalization relating constantly conjoined or regularly associated phenomena.

Statistical–probabilistic explanation

In the standard account, the 'covering laws' are held to describe events that are constantly conjoined. However, a modified version of this account includes explanations by implication from descriptions of high relative frequencies of association, in order to accommodate the forms of explanation common in the (supposedly less advanced) biological and social psychological sciences. Thus, for example, the descriptions 'the probability for persons exposed to the measles to catch the disease is high' and 'Tim was exposed to the measles' make it 'highly probable' that 'Tim caught the measles'. Analogously a case of aggression may be explained in terms of 'violent stimuli' by showing that the presence of violent stimuli rendered the aggressive action 'highly probable', given the description of a high relative frequency of association between violent stimuli and aggressive actions. This form of explanation is called 'statistical–probabilistic' (Hempel 1966).

Explanation and prediction

It is not surprising that this account appeals to the hard-nosed empiricist, who wants to restrict the business of science to the description of 'observables'. This is because it appears to satisfy the most rigorous requirements of scientific analysis without recourse to metaphysical obscurities such as 'power' and 'force'. The appeal may best be illustrated via the famous example from Molière, ridiculing the pompous pretensions of a scholastic doctor. The good doctor 'explains' why the ingestion of opium causes drowsiness by reference to the 'soporific power' of opium. But what does it mean to say that opium has 'soporific power'? Well it means that people who ingest opium become drowsy! Yet all is not lost. The good doctor further explains that the 'soporific power' of opium is grounded in its 'dormative nature'. But what does it mean to say that opium has a 'dormative nature'? Well, it means that people who ingest opium become drowsy!

A reference to causal 'power' can thus appear superfluous and circular. If it serves any explanatory function at all, it simply makes reference to constant or regular correlation between events such as opium ingestion and drowsiness, which alone is sufficient to explain phenomena such as drowsiness. Furthermore, a reference to such a correlation is entirely sufficient for the other two purposes of rigorous science: prediction and control. Given knowledge of the correlation between opium ingestion and drowsiness, we can predict when people will become drowsy (when they ingest opium) and make them drowsy (by making them ingest opium). Analogously we can predict and control instances of gas expansion, measles, and aggressive action via our knowledge of laws descriptive of correlations of these phenomena with antecedent instances of the heating of a gas, exposure to measles, and 'violent stimuli'. A reference to causal 'power' appears to provide no additional useful information to facilitate our ability to predict and control events and actions.

This account naturally leads to the close assimilation (if not identification) of explanation and prediction. Thus in the standard scientific empiricist account, explanation and prediction are held to be logically symmetrical, the only difference being the tense of the descriptions of the events and initial conditions. Thus from the covering law 'all heated gases expand' and the description of initial conditions 'the gas is being heated' one can predict that 'the gas will expand'. Analogously from covering laws describing statistical regularities and descriptions of initial conditions one can predict that it is 'highly probable' that persons will contract measles or become aggressive. So close is the assimilation of explanation and prediction that predictive success is treated as the acid test of the adequacy of a causal explanation (Hempel and Oppenheim 1948: 155). 'An explanation is not fully adequate unless its explanans, if taken account of in time, could have served as a basis for predicting the phenomena'.

This account has in turn been accepted by social psychological scientists to the degree that predictive utility is treated as an essential feature of a good explanation:

> Science is deterministic in its mode of reasoning since only deterministic assumptions give us licence to make predictions, and this we have already taken to be a distinguishing feature of scientific explanation in general.
>
> (Beloff 1973: 7)

Accidental correlation

Unfortunately this popular account of causality and causal explanation is dogged by a very serious problem, noted originally by Hume but not resolved by him or future generations of empiricists.

The regularity account of causality includes too much, since constant or regular correlation is not sufficient for a causal sequence. The regularity account also includes accidental correlations, where events may be constantly or regularly correlated but *not* causally related. Thus, for example, the motions of two spatially adjacent pendulums satisfy all the Humean conditions but their motions are causally independent of each other. The ringing of two spatially adjacent alarm clocks also satisfy these conditions, but no one in their right mind would suppose that the ringing of one causes the ringing of the other. Analogously, although a high correlation between violence in the media and in society may arise because violence in the media is a cause of violence in society, this may not be the case. It might be the case that the correlation holds because the two phenomena are joint effects of a further cause (e.g. a breakdown in social mores). And some correlations are purely accidental, resulting from, for example, accidental synchronization of cyclical phenomena. Thus it is well known that there is a high correlation between the PhD and mule populations in Southern California, but it is most unlikely that these phenomena are causally related in any way.

Non-explanatory prediction

The same problem affects the logical assimilation of explanation and prediction. For many descriptions of correlations may be enormously useful as predictive devices, but thoroughly bad explanations. Thus, for example, the high correlation between abnormal animal behaviour and earthquakes may enable us to successfully predict earthquakes, but a reference to abnormal animal behaviour is a thoroughly bad explanation of earthquakes. For centuries it was known that there is a high correlation between exposure to the noxious vapours from swamps and yellow fever, and this still serves as an excellent predictive device for anticipating instances of yellow fever. However, it does not provide a good explanation of yellow fever, for it is the bite of the tiger mosquito (and the virus it carries) that causes yellow fever and a reference to which provides the best explanation of yellow fever.

Now there have been numerous attempts to amend the empiricist account to distinguish between genuinely causal sequences and accidental correlation. There is little point considering these attempts because they are doomed to failure for the following simple reason. The empiricist wants but cannot have it both ways. He wants to deny that causality involves anything more than observable correlation, and in particular that it involves some mysterious 'power'. Yet he also wishes to retain the notion of 'real generation' to maintain the distinction between genuine causal sequences and purely accidental correlation. However, the empiricist cannot maintain the Humean or 'regularity' account and retain the traditional distinction. For either causality is nothing more than the constant conjunction of observables, in which case there is no distinction to be made between 'causal' and 'accidental' sequences, or there is a real difference between causal and accidental sequences, in which case causality cannot be equated with constant conjunction.

CAUSAL POWERS

There is another reason for not considering the tortuous attempts to maintain the regularity account and preserve the traditional distinction between causal and accidental correlation. For all these attempts are based upon the assumption that constant or regular correlation is a *necessary* but not a *sufficient* condition for causality. All such attempts involve the search for the 'surplus element' that distinguishes causal from accidental correlations.

However, this assumption is mistaken. It is not a necessary condition of a causal power that it be manifested in a constant or regular correlation. Cigarette smoking is a cause of lung cancer, but relatively few smokers get lung cancer. Plutonium 239 has the power to cause tissue damage and death by radiation, but mercifully few people get exposed to it without protection. There are stockpiled chemical weapons that have the power to annihilate whole populations, but thankfully no-one has yet suffered from exposure to them (at least until very recently). It cannot be assumed that the causal powers of particulars are manifested in constant or regular sequences because the causal powers of some particulars can be interfered with by the causal powers of other particulars. Thus prophylactics can prevent instances of a disease despite exposure to the bacillus that causes it.

The origins of this fundamental empiricist error are not difficult to trace. The original forms of empiricism – including Hume's – were *phenomenalist* in nature. It was held that we can have experience and knowledge only of our sense impressions (of colour, shape, size, texture, etc.). We cannot have knowledge of the properties of physical objects existing independently of our sense impressions because we have no sensory experience of them. The worth of this doctrine need not be considered here. What should be noted is that within this framework it is of course true that our knowledge of causality could only be knowledge of which complexes of sense impressions are regularly associated with others. For within this framework, that is all that can be known.

However, this phenomenalism was simply abandoned by later generations of empiricists. Those who called themselves scientific empiricists, including the behaviourist fathers of modern psychology, treated publicly-verifiable observations of the properties of physical objects as the epistemological foundation of science. Yet on the level of physical objects, there is no longer any epistemological justification for retaining the Humean account of causality, and a very good reason for rejecting it. For on this level, the causal powers of physical objects, persons, and social collectives must be recognized as not only constrained by their enabling and stimulus conditions (usually referenced in traditional empiricist accounts), but by the causal powers of other phenomena that may interfere with or impede their exercise (Geach 1975).

The realist conception of causality is based upon an ontology of 'powerful particulars' (acids, gravitational fields, persons, etc.) rather than the discarded empiricist ontology of sensory events (Harré and Madden 1975). This account locates the generative power of particulars in their natures, given local enabling and stimulus conditions. In the case of physical particulars, their nature is usually specified by reference to their intrinsic composition and structure. Thus, for example, the superconductive power of tin is explained in terms of long-range electron coupling, given a very low temperature (enabling condition) and application of a potential difference (stimulus condition). However, it is not assumed in this explanation that tin will always manifest this power when these conditions are satisfied, for this power can be interfered with by the presence of a local magnetic field.

A reference to the causal power of opium to generate drowsiness does enable us to explain why some agents get drowsy by reference to their prior ingestion of opium, despite the fact that some agents do not become drowsy after the ingestion of opium, because of a high tolerance level. A reference to the causal power of opium does not of course explain *why* opium causes drowsiness.

A reference to the nature of opium – a reference to its alkaloid molecular structure and receptor sites in the nervous system – does that.

Causal 'laws'

The realist does not suppose that there is some mysterious extra thing to be observed in a causal sequence, or referenced in a causal description. For the realist, descriptions of causal power are descriptions of what particulars can do, given their natures and local conditions. Given the possibility of interference, the realist denies that causal 'laws' can be analysed as descriptions of degrees of correlation. Causal 'laws' must be analysed as open-ended conditionals of the form 'if something has a certain nature and certain conditions are satisfied, then that thing will produce a certain effect, unless something interferes'.

The traditional empiricist account of causal descriptions is a natural consequence of the principle of meaning empiricism and the verification principle: according to this account, causal descriptions are naturally held to describe the observable correlations that confirm them. The realist recognizes that causal descriptions can only be confirmed by the observation of particular correlations that are manifestations of causal power, but denies that causal power descriptions or causal 'laws' are descriptions of degrees of correlation. Newton's first law is a classic example: 'all bodies continue in a state of rest, or of uniform motion in a right line, *unless* it is compelled to change that state by forces impressed upon it'. Although the only empirical support for this law is our observations of the correlated motions of moving bodies, the law does not describe any degree of correlation. In actual fact (strictly speaking) no bodies continue at rest or in a right line, or only few in relatively isolated systems.

Closed and open systems

The empiricist account of causality only holds true of the causal powers of particulars in ontologically *closed* systems: that is, systems in which particulars are isolated from possible interference (Bhaskar 1975). Thus, for example, it is only in the artificial confines of a laboratory vacuum experiment that it is true that all bodies fall with equal acceleration. In *open* systems outside the laboratory that are not isolated, different bodies – trucks, persons, chickens, hammers, feathers, and dust particles – fall with quite different accelerations, because of differences in air resistance. Furthermore although there are naturally-occurring closed systems, these *natural closures* are often epistemically open. That is, it is often only when we have some control over the relevant variables that we can have confidence that we have isolated the causal powers of a system.

This is not to say that non-laboratory sciences are doomed to causal ambiguity. Conditions of generation and interference (and functional relationships) can be determined by the careful comparison of naturally varying systems in which the relevant variables are carefully discriminated, as in the case of astronomy or ethology, for example. The interventive techniques of ontological isolation may be supplemented by logical isolation, by the observation of a naturally occurring or specially created control system.

Experimental isolation

Nevertheless the frequent dependence on laboratory intervention in natural and social psychological sciences forces us to recognize the inadequacies of the scientific empiricist account. The 'instance-statistics' account of confirmation is inadequate because it does not square with the methodological fact that causal powers in natural science are regularly established on the basis of relatively few closed experiments (Toulmin 1953), in which alternative hypothetical mechanisms of generation and interference are eliminated (Bhaskar 1975). If, under such conditions of closure, an isolated particular or structure manifests a certain effect, then the scientist has established that that particular or structure has the power to generate that effect. Thus, for example, if tin at a very low temperature manifests superconductivity when a potential difference is applied, then it has been established that tin has the power to act as a superconductor under these conditions. It has not been established that tin will invariably act as a superconductor given these conditions. Further varied experiments need to be done to determine conditions that may interfere with the exercise of this power, such as the presence of a magnetic field. Although it is true that experiments must be repeated, the point of this practice is not to accumulate further instance statistics. From a logical point of view, a single observation of an effect in an isolated system is sufficient to demonstrate that the isolated particular has the power to generate that effect. Experiments are repeated *to test the experiment*. If the experimental result is not repeated in further reproductions, the experiment is rejected as a failure to achieve experimental closure (since differential results indicate lack of control of some of the variables).

Correlation

In general the only constant or regular correlations relevant to the evaluation of causal claims are those produced in the artificial confines of closed experiments in scientific laboratories. In open systems outside of scientific laboratories there is only at most a very tenuous relationship between causality and correlation. The frequency with which a particular will manifest a causal power depends upon the contingent circumstance of how frequently interferences are co-present. This will vary from never to always. Thus the tubercle bacillus may rarely manifest its power to generate tuberculosis because of the almost universal distribution of prophylactive, but regrettably (at present) the rabies virus almost invariably generates nervous system destruction and death (after a short incubation period).

In consequence, degrees of open system correlation cannot be treated as any measure of the probability of a causal relationship, despite the fact that this is often appealed to as evidence prior to, or instead of, controlled laboratory experiments or field studies. Thus for example the fact that the condition of most neurotics improves consequent to psychotherapy does nothing to suggest the causal potency of psychotherapy, nor does the low incidence of aggression in children consequent to watching violent television cast doubt upon its causal potency. For psychotherapy and the improvement of neurotics may be accidentally correlated (if the passage of time is sufficient for remission in most cases (Eysenck 1952)), and the power of violent television to generate aggression in young children may be usually inhibited by parental or peer pressure.

Explanation and prediction

Another important feature of this realist analysis is that the utility of a causal explanation as a predictive device cannot be treated as a criterion of the adequacy of such an explanation. The causal powers of particulars can be established in closed experiments long before the scientist is in a position to anticipate generative and interference factors in open systems. For example the medical scientist may be able to identify the viral cause of a disease long before she can anticipate contact and resistance. A non-explanatory description of a *de facto* correlation in open systems may often be a far better predictor of events than an explanatory reference to the causal powers of a particular. Thus a reference to an early disease syndrome may be a better predictor of instances of a disease than a well-established explanatory reference to contact with a bacillus (Harré 1972).

It might be objected that the distinction between causal explanations and descriptions of accidental correlation can be accommodated by a modification of the traditional empiricist account of explanation. It might be claimed that we can discriminate causal explanatory from accidental correlations by requiring that the antecedent factors specified in the correlation – which may be high or low – increase the probability of the consequent event (Salmon 1971). Thus for example we might dismiss a causal explanation of the recovery of neurotics by reference to psychotherapy because the employment of psychotherapy does not increase the probability of improvement (relative to persons who receive no psychotherapy), despite the relatively high correlation. Or we might recognize the adequacy of the causal explanation of lung cancer in terms of cigarette smoking because it increases the probability of a person's getting lung cancer (relative to non-smokers), despite the low correlation.

However, we should be very careful to distinguish the reasonable requirement that adequate causal explanations be confirmed by a comparative analysis of experimentally produced or naturally occurring systems, from the unreasonable requirement that causal explanations be expressed as correlations (high or low) that increase the probability of a certain effect. There are many factors (which may be described in terms of high or low correlation) that increase the probability of an event, but do not furnish a correct causal explanation of it. A stay in hospital increases the probability of death but is only rarely a cause of it. The presence of noxious vapours from swamps and abnormal animal behaviour increase the probability of cases of yellow fever and earthquakes but do not cause them. The polio vaccine *decreases* the probability of polio in agents who receive it (relative to those who do not), but is unfortunately the cause of polio in some (albeit rare) cases.

Explanation and description

These considerations require us to make a fundamental distinction between *causal-explanatory* and *descriptive–correlative* propositions. Causal-explanatory propositions are based upon the causal powers of particulars and are expressed as qualified conditionals concerned with *possibilities*. In most natural sciences, they describe what *would* happen given certain (enabling and stimulus) conditions unless something interferes. They are established by invariant correlations under conditions of closure (invariant correlation under conditions of closure is sufficient to demonstrate a causal power).[1] Degrees of correlation in open systems are quite irrelevant to the evaluation of causal-explanatory propositions (correlation in open systems is neither necessary nor sufficient for their confirmation). The main purpose of such propositions is causal explanatory inference to open systems. Thus, for example, if it has been established under conditions of closure that tiger mosquito bites cause yellow fever and that 'violent stimuli' cause aggressive actions, then instances of yellow fever and aggression in open systems can be explained by reference to antecedent instances of tiger mosquito bites and violent stimuli.

Descriptive correlative propositions are based upon contingent distributions of conditions of generation and interference and are expressed as statistical generalizations concerned with *actualities*: they describe the actual degree of correlation of any two phenomena at any time or place, whether these phenomena be causally or accidentally correlated. Thus propositions describing a high (or low) degree of correlation in open systems between tiger mosquito bites and yellow fever, smoking and lung cancer, disease syndromes and diseases, abnormal animal behaviour and earthquakes, hospitalization and death, and mule and Ph.D. populations in Southern California are all descriptive correlative propositions. Such propositions are confirmed by reference to sample estimates in open systems, and their degree of confirmation is proportional to the size and representative nature of the sample. The purpose of such propositions is probabilistic prediction in open systems. Given a high (or low) correlation between two factors, the probability of one factor given the other is high (or low).

While these points may require us to modify the traditional analysis of causal explanation in social psychological science, they also enable us to answer many of the traditional criticisms. Objections based upon the claim that there are few constant or regular correlations to be determined by social psychological science, or that social psychological explanations are poor predictors of human action, simply miss the mark because correlation in open systems is no measure of the adequacy of causal explanations. If it is the case that the power of an authority (perceived as competent) to generate 'destructive obedience' can be established in closed laboratory experiments (Milgram 1974), then instances of 'destructive obedience' in open systems (the 'real world' outside the laboratory) can be adequately explained by reference to antecedent instances of authoritarian commands. The adequacy of this explanation does not entail that these phenomena are constantly or regularly correlated, for authoritarian commands can be resisted given moral support from peers. Nor does the adequacy of this explanation entail that such actions can be predicted in open systems, for it may be extremely difficult to anticipate conditions of generation and interference. Given the enormous difficulties of predicting events in open systems (over which we have no control), we have no more right to doubt the worth of the explanations advanced by social psychological scientists because or their predictive failures than we have to blame our family doctor or the experimental physicist for failing to predict our summer cold or the trajectory or a leaf that blows in our window.

This is not of course to deny that increased knowledge of conditions of generation and interference improves our ability to anticipate physical events and human actions. It is merely to stress that the adequacy of a causal explanation entirely depends upon the quality of the observational discrimination of causal powers under conditions of closure, and not upon the predictive utility of any descriptive correlation. It is also worth noting that more often than not the dividend of increased causal knowledge is more successful intervention rather than superior prediction. For example our determination of the tubercle bacillus as the cause of tuberculosis, and our determination of the structure of the tubercle bacillus, enabled medical scientists to develop the antibiotic streptomycin. The dividend of this knowledge was the *elimination* of the historically prior regular correlation between exposure to the tubercle bacillus and tuberculosis, not the prediction of a correlation.

tion. This example also gives the lie to the empiricist complaint about the superfluity of explanatory references to the *natures* of particulars.

This point is particularly important to stress, because critics of social psychological science regularly confuse issues of explanatory adequacy with issues concerning correlation. Thus, for example, Gergen (1973) characterizes social psychological sciences as 'historical' disciplines, because the correlations that held in the past may no longer hold today. Thus, for example, the frequency of 'bystander apathy' may be greatly reduced when persons learn of the phenomenon. The high degree of conformity manifested in Asch's 1950s experiments (Asch 1951) is (apparently) not manifested in contemporary reproductions (Perrin and Spencer 1980). However, the (perhaps greatly) reduced frequency of 'bystander apathy' does not undermine the explanation based upon the numbers of other bystanders present, established by laboratory and field experiments (Latané and Darley 1970). A reference to the number of other bystanders may still provide an entirely adequate explanation of the (perhaps very) rare instances of 'bystander apathy', just as the very rare cases of tuberculosis can still be explained by reference to exposure to the tubercle bacillus. Analogously the reduced frequency of conformity in contemporary reproductions of Asch's experiments may simply be due to the increased resistance to group pressure among individuals in the 1980s. The group pressures may still be present and may provide an entirely adequate explanation of the perhaps rare cases of conformity.

Of course these are properly empirical questions, and it is not denied that the causal powers of physical particulars, persons, and social collectives can change (or wax and wane) over time and place, as the nature of particulars, persons, and collectives change. The powers of a disease bacillus may become eliminated (or attenuated or strengthened) given biochemical changes in the structure of the bacillus. The powers of persons may be altered given changes in social relations and representations (or neurophysiology). It is simply stressed that the answer to these questions cannot be determined by reference to degrees of correlation in open systems.

HUMAN AGENCY

It is commonly supposed that causal explanations of human actions are inconsistent with our everyday assumption that many human actions are the product of human *agency*: that is, that they are *self-determined* by agents in accord with their avowed reasons. Yet although some causal explanations are inconsistent with some agency explanations, it is not the case that a commitment to the causal explanation of human action precludes the recognition of human agency.

An explanation of an action in terms of human agency involves the claim that the action was self-determined by the agent, rather than being determined by any conditions, including the psychological states of the agent. Such explanations imply that the agent (at least sometimes) has a *free choice* in deciding which course of action to engage in from a number of possible courses of action.

Causality and determinism

It is often said that agency explanations are inconsistent with the principle of universal causal generation. They are not. An agency explanation makes the claim that an action was causally generated by the agent, but denies that there were any conditions sufficient to determine the agent to do one thing rather than another. Agency explanations are, however, inconsistent with the principle of universal causal *determinism*, which states that for every physical event or human action there is a set of conditions that is ontologically *sufficient* for the generation of the event or action.

Now it is also often said that the principle of universal causal determinism is a presupposition of all scientific enquiry. However, it is most doubtful if many practising scientists (including social psychological scientists) are in fact committed to this principle. Most scientists believe that many physical processes and human actions can be brought within the *control* of the scientist, as a result of practical intervention. They believe (with justification) that many interventions are effective, and that it is up to them to *choose* whether such interventions will or ought to be made. The natural scientist, for example, may be a determinist about death but not disease, because he believes he has the ability and the choice to intervene in the case of disease. As noted earlier, it is precisely the ability to intervene that enables many scientists to conduct experiments.

There is another reason why many natural scientists are not committed to universal causal determinism. This is because this principle has in fact been abandoned on the level of quantum mechanical explanations. Furthermore it is simply not true that this principle is a logical presupposition of scientific enquiry (whatever individual scientists believe). The only requirement for scientific enquiry is that the phenomena explained be locatable in an objective and unified spacio-temporal order: there must be some way of determining the objective time order of events as opposed to the subjective order in which we experience them.[2] The principle of universal causal generation does this job by precluding the conceptual possibility of purely *spontaneous* events: events for which it is true that other events or conditions play *no* role in their generation. It is not necessary – although it is sufficient – to employ the principle of universal causal determinism for this purpose. We need not suppose that for each event there is a set of conditions sufficient to generate it. It is sufficient for the purpose of locating events in an objective and unified spacio-temporal order that we make the *weaker* assumption that some events have enabling conditions only: conditions that are necessary for the production of an event but which are (on at least some occasions) not jointly sufficient for the production of the event.

Suppose for the sake of argument that the firing of some nerve cells is undetermined, that there are no conditions sufficient to determine the firing of the cell. Suppose also, however, that there are some enabling conditions that are necessary for the firing of the nerve cell, such as reaching a certain electrical potential. This latter (and much weaker) supposition is enough to enable us to locate nerve-cell firings in an objective and unified spacio-temporal order: they always follow the achievement of a certain electrical potential because they *must*, since the achievement of a certain electrical potential is a necessary enabling condition for the firing of a nerve cell. Furthermore, under these circumstances, we can give a perfectly proper causal explanation of the firing of nerve cells (when they do fire) in terms of how they are enabled to fire by the raising of the electrical potential. This is in fact the sort of explanation that is standardly given of certain sub-atomic phenomena, such as radioactivity.

Essentially the same point may be made in the following

fashion. The empiricist account of causality precludes agency explanations because it analyses causal explanation in terms of the constant or invariant conjunction of events. The inadequacies of this account have already been noted. A realist account of causality allows the possibility of agency explanations because it analyses causality in terms of the powers of particulars. According to this account, to attribute a causal power to a physical particular or person is simply to say that it *can* generate a certain effect, not that it will or must.

Natural and human powers

The natural sciences rarely countenance purely spontaneous events. It is usually presumed that events have at least necessary enabling conditions, and many of these have in fact been discriminated (e.g. the presence of oxygen is necessary for combustion). Even this claim must, however, be qualified, for some theories do countenance purely spontaneous events (such as the spontaneous generation of matter or energy), and some would argue that we must countenance such events on pain of an infinite regress with respect to our explanations.

It is also true that although natural sciences do countenance events on the sub-atomic level that may have enabling conditions only, centuries of natural scientific experience have led most scientists to the justified conclusion that the powers of many physical particulars have *stimulus conditions*, since many of these have in fact been discriminated. This enables us to say in the case of tin, for example, that given a very low temperature it *will* act as a superconductor when a potential difference is applied, and that it *must* given its physical nature and local conditions.

However, there is no such presumption in the case of human powers, such as the abilities to speak French, play the piano, solve logical theorems, fly an aircraft, teach chemistry, maintain calm in an emergency, and recognize the signs of child abuse and the early symptoms of AIDS, and it is hard to imagine putative stimulus conditions for such powers. The presence of another French speaker or a piano are most naturally conceived as *opportunities* for the exercise of powers such as the ability to speak French or play the piano, rather than stimulus conditions that are sufficient to determine French utterances or musical performances. We are not usually determined or driven to speak French or play the piano (although on occasions we may be). Rather we exploit or fail to exploit opportunities.

Accordingly we do not say of the woman with the ability to speak French or play the piano that she will speak French or play the piano when faced with another French speaker or a piano, far less that she must. Rather we say that she *may* exercise these powers given these opportunities, or she *may not*.

The critical difference between natural and human powers is that the exercise of a human power is within the *control* of the agent. The power of tin to act as a superconductor is not within the control of samples of tin, and of course it makes no sense to talk this way. The power of an agent to speak French or play the piano is entirely within the control of the agent if she has this power. Given an opportunity for its exercise, an agent can act or *refrain from acting* according to her personal reasons.

Of course the everyday assumptions of social agents prove nothing. The point that is presently stressed is that there is nothing prescientific or unscientific about such assumptions, and that they are not in any way in conflict with the causal-explanatory goals of social psychological science. The well-established fact that many natural-scientific phenomena can be given causal explanations in terms of stimulus conditions does not entail that the same will hold true in the realm of human action. The concept of causal power does not vouchsafe this in either the natural or social psychological domain.

Human liabilities

This is not to deny that some human actions may be determined by stimulus conditions that are sufficient to generate them. Undoubtedly some are. We already have reasonable empirical and experimental grounds for supposing that 'violent stimuli' may be sufficient to produce aggression in some persons, and that the presence of other bystanders may be sufficient to produce apathy in some persons faced with an emergency. The agent may be driven to suicide and may be unable to desist when she represents her miscarriage as a personal failure. Nevertheless it is a wholly ungrounded metaphysical act of faith to presume that all human actions can be explained in such terms.

Significantly, with respect to such actions we are more inclined to talk about *human liabilities* rather than human powers, because they are stimulus bound and not within the agent's control. Thus we say that some agents are liable to be apathetic in an emergency when other bystanders are present, even if they have good reasons for intervening. We say that some persons are liable to be aggressive when presented with 'violent stimuli', even if they have good reasons to desist. We say that some persons are liable to continue smoking even though they may try everything in their power to prevent themselves.

Of course the degree to which human actions are determined by stimulus conditions or are self-determined products of agency is an empirical question. The point to be stressed is precisely that it is an empirical question. The postulation of stimulus conditions is a useful methodological goal in experimental social psychological science, both to establish particular stimulus conditions and to press the limits of this form of explanation. However, it cannot be presumed that there will always be such conditions to be determined. If we do not find social or psychological or neurophysiological conditions (or some combination thereof) that are sufficient to generate particular forms of action, then we ought not to doubt the adequacy of our social psychological science if we come to conclude that there are no such conditions (just as we ought not to conclude that our physical science is inadequate when we are forced to conclude this with respect to natural-scientific phenomena, such as radioactivity).

CAUSALITY AND MEANING

The above discussion has taken pains to stress that a causal explanatory science of human action does not preclude explanations in terms of human agency. It is equally important to stress that the socially meaningful nature of human action does not vouchsafe any explanations in terms of human agency. For it is most unfortunate that those theorists who stress the meaningful nature of human action often seem to suppose that this entails that the best (or the only) explanation that can be given of socially meaningful actions is in terms of human agency. It is unfortunate because this is one of the main reasons why many researchers are disinclined to embrace questions of meaning and purpose, because they feel that a recognition of the meaningful nature of human action prejudges explanatory questions in favour of human agency.

In fact it does not, as noted in Chapter 1. This is because a recognition of the meaningful nature of human action does not prejudge *any* explanatory questions, far less prejudge them in favour of human agency. The recognition that most human actions are socially located and intentionally directed leaves entirely open the question of their best explanation. Thus the best explanation of intentionally directed acts of aggression may be that they are causally determined by specific brain states. The best explanation of socially located acts of conformity may be in terms of peer pressures that are sufficient to determine them. The best explanation of some acts of aggression or conformity may be in terms of determination by brain states or peer pressures, and other acts of aggression or conformity may be best explained as self-determined acts of revenge or expediency.

AGENCY AND MEANING

Although the socially meaningful nature of human action does not vouchsafe explanations in terms of human agency, the social dimensions of psychological states that provide agent reasons for action do strongly suggest the *plausibility* of some explanations in terms of human agency.

The ideal of many contemporary cognitive scientists is the explanation of human actions in terms of psychologically internalized rules and reasons which, given appropriate environmental inputs, are *sufficient* to generate human actions. Thus, for example, Fodor (1975: 74) claims that: '... a representation of the rules they [i.e. organisms] follow constitutes one of the causal determinants of their behaviour'.

However, rules, reasons, and values are intrinsically social entities. They are not the mere aggregation of individual representations of rules, reasons, and values, but are historically-located products of evolving social negotiation and consensus. The contents of the rules, reasons, and values followed by individual agents are 'appropriated' by individual agents in the course of their development (Vygotsky 1962), and developed by them to cope with the particular exigencies of their life experience. Like the theories of natural science, they must of necessity be 'partially interpreted' (Hempel 1965) or 'open-horizoned' (Waismann 1945) so that indeterminate potentialities for meaning change and development can be actualized to accommodate novel facts or features of reality.

Social representations of rules do not specify 'how to go on' beyond the standard situations that form the basis of social consensus and social learning (Wittgenstein 1953). The socially evolved consensus determines the limits of legitimate transformations, and develops through social negotiation to accommodate novel forms of social life. Thus one-parent 'families' may be accepted as families but homosexual 'marriages' may not be accepted as marriages.

The open-ended nature of social representations not only allows for the development of social meaning in reaction to novelty and change. It also provides for the development of *personal meaning* in the production of action. The social consensus covers the standard situations, but the agent must decide for herself how to act in novel and difficult situations. She must decide for herself whether another's action is aggressive, dishonest, or disobedient in non-standard situations, and she must decide for herself how to interpret social rules in novel and difficult situations, and then act in accord with her individual interpretation. As Margolis notes (1984: 90): 'Language is ... incapable of being formulated as a closed system of rules; subject always to the need for improvisational interpretation, and, therefore, subject also to ineliminable psychological indeterminacies regarding intention and action'.

Such partially interpreted rules can and must be developed by agents in the light of their own personal experience. Representations of reasons that may be treated by agents as *sufficient reasons* for action cannot invariably function as *sufficient conditions* for action, since such reason representations do not invariably specify determinate action outcomes even in fairly specific circumstances. Human action often appears undetermined by reasons because various courses of action may be held to be in accordance with the agent's reasons.

Thus the agent may wish to do his duty, but finds it hard to determine whether this is best served by going off to fight for the Free French or staying with his mother, as in Sartre's (1948) famous example. The agent may wish to help his brother who is accused of rape, but finds it difficult to decide whether his brother's interest is best served by informing the social services or providing him with an alibi.

From the cognitive science perspective, we may note that agents do (and must) employ theories in order to make their way in the social world. These theories must be 'partially interpreted' in order that they may be developed to deal with novelties and difficulties. The scientist must determine how a 'partially interpreted' theory is to be developed if she is to continue as a scientist. We have to surmount the indeterminacies of social meaning if we are to make personal passages in the social world. As many existentialist philosophers have stressed, decisions about the development of social meaning often involve considerations of deep personal significance. In deciding whether to marry and move or stay at home and help save an ailing family business, one has to make 'strong evaluations' about the relative worth of courses of action that are intrinsic components of human 'identity projects'. We may bemoan the fact that social rules do not resolve these linguistically informed dilemmas, but we determine our identities by the individual ways in which we resolve them or refuse to face them.

Agency and social psychological science

The possibility and plausibility of human agency has been argued for at some length in order to defuse a very popular but misguided objection to the scientific analysis of socially meaningful human action: namely that a commitment to human agency or freedom somehow precludes the causal explanation of human action. It has been argued that it does not. The recognition of the plausibility and possibility of human agency does require some modification of the traditional conception of social psychological science and its goals. However, also contrary to the conventional wisdom of both critics and defenders of social psychological science, it does not require any modification (or any major modification) of its experimental and empirical practice.

Contemporary social psychological science does not in fact establish or investigate the 'determinants' of human action, nor does it pretend to. The notion that it does is pure science fiction (or science fantasy). Even those avowedly concerned to investigate the stimulus conditions that precipitate the manifestation of human liabilities do not generally suppose that such conditions are sufficient to determine human actions: they are rather conceived as powerful influences that promote certain forms of action, but which may be resisted or surmounted by individuals.

Certainly it is rarely the case for example that researchers predict that stimulus conditions such as 'violent stimuli' will generate aggressive actions in all those subjects exposed to them in the experimental group. They only predict that the incidence of aggressive actions (or degree of aggression according to some measure of the degree of injury intended) will be greater in the experimental group 'exposed' to 'violent stimuli' than in a control group not 'exposed' to such stimulus conditions.[3] That is, even with respect to the experimental analysis of human liabilities, researchers are only concerned with conditions that promote or impede certain forms of action, that incline us to act (or think) in certain ways or discourage us from acting (or thinking) in these ways. Only when they are momentarily in the grip of standard empiricist rhetoric do they claim otherwise. This rhetoric is not, however, reflected in their practice, which is entirely consistent with a recognition of human agency.

Furthermore most social psychological research (with the exception of clinical psychological research) is not much concerned with the stimulus conditions for human liabilities. It is concerned to establish the neurophysiological, psychological, and social enabling conditions – both local and developmental – of human powers such as the abilities to use language, be an effective teacher, understand mathematics and logical form, recognize emergencies and child abuse, and form stable relationships with peers and intimates, and the conditions that promote or impede their effective exercise. Theoretical claims about such enabling (and promoting or impeding) conditions are confirmed by the comparative analysis of experimental or naturally occurring systems in which these conditions are present or absent or differ in degrees, to determine whether observed differences in performance may be explained in these terms. These claims are of course entirely consistent with a recognition of human agency, as are the forms of empirical enquiry employed to assess them. Such enabling conditions are not determinants of human action: they only determine the limits and potential of human action. Only someone wholly bewitched by empiricist rhetoric would be even tempted to suggest otherwise.

PREDICTION AND CONTROL

The real possibility of human agency does delimit the traditionally avowed goal of social psychological science as the prediction and control of human action. However, two points should be noted immediately. First, the prediction of events in open systems is an unrealistic goal for most sciences. The natural sciences are not significantly more successful in this area than social psychological science. In fact, insofar as many actions are based upon socially conventional rules and reasons, social psychological scientists and lay agents are often *better* at open-system prediction (especially extended predictions) than medical practitioners and meteorologists. We know very well what most people do at traffic lights and what trade unionists do when faced with insultingly low wage offers. Second, to attribute agency to humans is not to say that their actions will be random and unpredictable. Insofar as agents do act upon social rules and reasons, their actions will be predictable to the same high degree, even if they are products of agency. To attribute agency is only to claim that the agent has the power to refrain from particular forms of action. It is not to say that he will or is likely to do things that appear irrational and inappropriate to him in the light of his reasons and values.

As noted earlier, the dividend of causal knowledge is more often than not more successful intervention rather than more successful prediction. Our knowledge of the enabling conditions of human powers, and of the stimulus and interference conditions of human liabilities, enables social psychological scientists to encourage or discourage various forms of action in the social world. Thus we may promote mathematical and social skills in children and adults by creating conditions that enable them to be developed. We may deter acts of aggression by reducing exposure to 'violent stimuli' (via media regulation or gun control) or by demonstrating our public willingness to punish acts of aggression (either collectively or individually). We may encourage altruistic actions by enabling agents to surmount their liability to 'bystander apathy' by means of education, or we may discourage destructive actions through psychotherapy designed to enable agents to surmount this liability.

This does create a problem for the traditional account of prediction and control, for it locates a tension between these two goals. Interventions based upon causal knowledge that extend human powers and eliminate or alleviate human liabilities increase the capacity for *self-control* of actions by lay agents, rather than increasing the capacity of social psychological scientists to control human actions. In consequence, the practical interventions of social psychological scientists generally render human action less predictable than before, by opening up *new possibilities* of action for agents.

Furthermore, given our already substantial social achievements with respect to the prediction of human action, we might wonder how these achievements could be extended. The only way the social psychological scientist could approximate the goal of ever increasing predictive adequacy is by exercising greater control over social agents in open systems, by controlling the dissemination of social psychological knowledge, by manipulating the stimulus conditions for human liabilities, and by delimiting the opportunities and options for self-determined action. Thus, for example, we could no doubt more successfully predict instances of 'destructive obedience' by strengthening authorities and reducing the information and moral support from peers available to many social agents.

Perhaps no-one would seriously suggest that we should do this. I certainly hope not. Nevertheless it is gratuitously assumed by many psychologists that 'potentially beneficial' regularities identified in laboratory experiments should be recreated by the manipulation of agents in open systems (Henschel 1980). By focusing on the question of which individuals or authorities should make the necessary value judgements and exercise the necessary control (Skinner 1974), many theorists simply avoid the question of whether such external control of human actions *should* be exercised.

It should be stressed that there are no reasons intrinsic to science for answering this question in the affirmative. Certainly there are no reasons to be gleaned from an analysis of causal explanation or the requirements of scientific explanation. Our theoretical explanations of the causal generation of natural events and human actions do not dictate to us how such causal knowledge should be exploited. The latter question is an entirely separate *moral* and *political* question.

This is not of course to deny that there may often be very good moral or political reasons for social psychological intervention in the open system of the social world. This is often the case, for example, when destructive and dangerous actions threaten the social fabric and individual lives. It is rather to stress that decisions to intervene can only be justified by moral and political reasons. They are not vouchsafed by any scientific analysis of human action.

4

THEORY AND OBSERVATION

For many years, 'theory' was a dirty word in psychological science. In an attempt to completely disassociate their new discipline from philosophy, many psychologists shied away from all things speculative. They proposed to establish the scientific credentials of psychology by focusing exclusively on the 'observable'. Ironically this meant banishing discourse about psychological states from the realm of psychological science, since such states were held to be paradigm cases of things that are not intersubjectively observable. This is perhaps most obvious in the case of behaviourist psychologists, but it also remains true for most other psychologists (including cognitive, social, clinical, and developmental), who continue to insist upon the *operational definition* of theoretical terms that make apparent reference to psychological states.

Unfortunately there never was any good reason for this anti-theoretical stance. Certainly it was not based upon the practice of natural science, which has been increasingly theoretical (and increasingly successful) since the time of the Ancient Greeks and Babylonians. Ironically this peculiar stance is itself based upon certain philosophical principles long since abandoned by most philosophers and natural scientists (and it is doubtful if the latter ever adopted them). To understand this, one must look to the conceptual history of modern psychology.

EMPIRICISM

Psychological and meaning empiricism

Once again the *bête noire* in this story is the empiricist philosopher David Hume. Like his predecessors Locke and Berkeley, Hume was committed to the doctrine of *psychological empiricism*, according to which all our concepts or 'ideas' have their origin in sense experience. Thus to employ familiar examples, the psychological empiricist will claim that a blind man cannot have the concept of 'red', and that a person can only form the concept of 'table' if they have seen and touched examples of tables. The empiricist philosophers gave this doctrine a special *idealist* or *phenomenalist* twist by claiming that we cannot have sensory experience or knowledge of physical objects. They avowed that we can only experience and have knowledge of our individual sense impressions: for example, our sense impressions of colour, shape, texture, etc. In consequence they held that our concepts or 'ideas' of 'physical objects' such as 'tables' and 'trees' refer only to the 'constancy and coherence' of complexes of sense impressions of colour, shape, texture, etc., and not to actual tables and trees existing independently of our perception of them.

Now this doctrine is more or less a logical consequence of the eighteenth-century account of cognition. This account assumes the essential *homogeneity* of sensation and cognition: concepts or 'ideas' were held to differ from sense impressions in degree but not in kind, for they were held to be 'copies' or 'faint images' of sense impressions. Thus Hume, for example, held that concepts and beliefs differ from sense impressions only in terms of their weaker 'force and liveliness'.

Given this assumption it is not surprising that they believed that all concepts are derived from sense experience (or else make reference to the complex forms of our sense experience), for without sensory experience there could be no material for image formation. Nor is it surprising that this assumption spawned the principle of *meaning empiricism*. According to this principle, a concept or its linguistic expression in a description is meaningful if and only if it can be defined in terms of observables. Thus for example the concepts of redness and table, and the linguistic descriptions 'red' and 'table' can only be meaningfully employed to characterize instances of redness and tables if their employment is based upon prior sensory experience of instances of redness and tables. The operation of this principle is clear in Hume's account of causality, for example. According to Hume, the concept of 'cause' can only be meaningfully employed to refer to those aspects of our experience of causal sequences (spacial and temporal contiguity, priority of the cause, and 'constant conjunction' in experience) from which the concept is abstracted. If it is (mistakenly and illegitimately) supposed to make reference to some mysterious additional and unobservable thing then it is meaningless.

Logical positivism and scientific empiricism

The principle of meaning empiricism also underlies the *logical positivist* analysis of scientific theories. The logical positivists were committed to the *verification principle* (Schlick 1936), according to which the meaning of a proposition is to be identified with its method of verification by sensory experience. Accordingly the logical positivists declared that scientific theories making apparent reference to unobservable entities such as atoms or motives are meaningless unless their meaning is specified via 'correspondence rules' or 'operational definitions' that relate 'theoretical postulates' (or axioms) and 'observational laws' (or 'empirical theorems'). Thus, for example, it was held that the meaning of the postulates in the kinetic theory of gases that make apparent reference to molecules in random motion is specified by correspondence rules relating such propositions to the various gas laws specifying functional relations between the pressure, temperature, and volume of a gas (for example, by relating 'mean kinetic energy' and 'temperature'). According to such accounts the 'observational level' of scientific language is held to confer meaning on the 'theoretical level' by a process analogous to capillary action, involving an 'upward seepage' of meaning from the 'soil' of observational experience (Feigl 1970).

In the early *sensationalist* version of logical positivism, 'molecular' propositions about everyday physical objects – such as tables and trees – and postulated theoretical entities – such as atoms and motives – were held to be 'logical constructions' out of 'atomic' or 'protocol' sentences describing private 'sense data' (Carnap 1928: Neurath 1932). This account was essentially a modern formalization of classical empiricism. A basic tenet of the foundationalist epistemology of classical empiricism is the doctrine that our self-knowledge of sense-impressions is epistemologically privileged: sense-impressions are the only phenomena we have *certain* knowledge of. Our knowledge of tables and trees and atoms and motives was held to be an uncertain theoretical inference based upon sense-impressions.

Concerned with the consequences of an epistemological

foundation for science that is not intersubjectively verifiable (sense-data can be observed only by the individuals who experience them), the later positivists defined the atomic level of scientific language in terms of descriptions of the properties of publicly observable physical objects. This doctrine came to be known as *physicalism,* and positivists who avowed this doctrine came to characterize themselves as *logical empiricists* or *scientific empiricists.*

The sensationalist version of logical positivism provided the philosophical grounding for the introspective psychology of Wundt (1896) and Titchener (1897): the experimental investigation via private 'introspection' of the 'elements' of sensory experience. The physicalist version of positivism known as logical or scientific empiricism provided the philosophical grounding for the behaviourism of Tolman (1932) and Hull (1943):[1] the experimental analysis of publicly observable behaviour. This latter account survives in the standard scientific empiricist account of theoretical explanation. According to this account, empirical laws correlating 'observables' are explained by the deduction of descriptions of such correlations from a set of 'theoretical postulates' related to the observational level by 'correspondence rules' or 'operational definitions' (Braithwaite 1953; Hempel 1965; Nagel 1961).

This account maintains a linguistically objective analysis of 'observational laws': such propositions are held to be true or false according to whether they accurately describe *de facto* empirical correlations. However, it involves a rejection of any linguistically objective analysis of 'theoretical postulates': propositions about atoms and motives are not held to be true or false according to whether atoms and motives exist and have the properties our theoretical descriptions ascribe to them. An *instrumentalist* account of theoretical propositions is advocated. Theoretical propositions putatively 'about' atoms and motives are not held to make reference to atoms and motives and their properties, but are rather held to refer indirectly to the empirical laws in terms of which they are defined. Such propositions do not serve any additional referential functions. Rather they are intellectual constructions that serve as linguistic instruments for the 'conceptual integration' of empirical laws (Hempel 1965).

This doctrine is held to be a simple consequence of the thesis of meaning empiricism. It is held that propositions putatively 'about' atoms and motives cannot function as meaningful descriptions *of* atoms and motives, because the meaning of such propositions cannot be ostensively defined: we cannot grasp the meaning of such propositions by making observations of atoms or motives. If such propositions are to be meaningful, they must be defined in terms of empirical laws relating observables. Such propositions have no sense or reference independent of the empirical laws in terms of which they are defined.

Despite the popularity of this familiar account of theoretical propositions, it is not without its problems. The most serious criticisms have led to the development of various forms of *neo-empiricism*, including both *radical behaviourism* and *cognitive psychology*. These criticisms have also led to the development of a *relativist* philosophy of science, which forms part of the philosophical grounding of *social constructionism*. Despite their apparent differences, all these frameworks are essentially modifications of the standard empiricist account, and all strongly preserve the principle of meaning empiricism.

NEO-EMPIRICISM

Radical behaviourism

One of the central problems of the traditional empiricist account of scientific theory concerns its ability to provide an adequate account of theoretical explanation. If the meaning of theoretical propositions really is specified in terms of correspondence rules relating such propositions to empirical laws, it is very hard to understand how a reference to such propositions can provide any illuminating explanation of empirical laws. If the information content of theoretical propositions is wholly specified by the empirical laws that serve as their definiens, then a reference to theoretical propositions only repeats the information contained in the empirical laws. As Kimble (1989: 495) has recently noted, if 'intervening variables' in psychological science are operationally defined in terms of the empirical laws to which they bring conceptual integration, any putative explanation of empirical laws in terms of intervening variables would be viciously circular. Thus if 'schizophrenia', for example, is defined in terms of an observable behavioural syndrome, a reference to schizophrenia can hardly be advanced as an illuminating explanation of that syndrome.

This suggests the essential redundancy of theoretical terms. In a famous paper Craig (1956) demonstrated that the empirical content of a theory could survive the elimination of theoretical terms. This demonstration is hardly surprising since the whole content of a theory is defined in terms of its empirical law consequences in the first place. The problem about the potential redundancy of theory was clearly recognized by Hempel in his articulation of the 'theoretician's dilemma':

> If the terms and principles of a theory serve their purpose, that is, they establish definite connections among observable phenomena, then they can be dispensed with, since any chain of laws and interpretative statements establishing such a connection should then be replaceable by a law that directly links observational antecedents to observational sequents.
>
> (Hempel 1965: 186)

Whatever else one says about B.F. Skinner, one has to give him credit for grasping the nettle of this implication. His anti-theoretical stance is soundly based upon the logical redundancy of theoretical terms *given this account of theoretical meaning*. Skinner (1953, 1974) rejects all references to psychological states as spurious 'explanatory fictions' and 'exhausting digressions', and maintains that psychologists should focus their enquiries exclusively upon observable behaviours and their observable environmental determinants. In this respect he is perhaps the purest and most consistent representative of scientific empiricism.

Cognitive psychology

Few psychologists, and indeed relatively few behaviourists have been inclined to follow Skinner down this radical road. Most are inclined to the view that the intellectual constructions of scientific theory do serve a useful role *with respect to the prediction of novel empirical laws*. This was the attitude adopted by Tolman and the later Hull, for example, which eventually enabled liberalized forms of behaviourism to develop into cognitive psychology.

Most psychologists have essentially adopted Hempel's own solution to the 'theoretician's dilemma'. According to Hempel (1965), not all theoretical postulates are wholly defined in terms of the empirical laws to which they bring conceptual integration. Scientific theories are 'partially interpreted systems' which can be further interpreted to generate novel predictions on the observational level.

The classic expression of this instrumental justification of theory with respect to psychological science is to be found in MacCorquodale and Meehl's (1948) distinction between 'intervening variables' and 'hypothetical constructs'. According to MacCorquodale and Meehl (1948: 107), with respect to intervening variables, '... the statement of such a concept does not contain any words which are not reducible to the empirical laws'. Hypothetical constructs, on the other hand, involve 'words which are not reducible to the empirical laws'. While it is generally agreed that intervening variables are essentially redundant and eliminable, it is argued that hypothetical constructs are essential in a developing science. This account also provides the standard justification for the theoretical constructs of cognitive psychology (Anderson 1981; Lachman, Lachman, and Butterfield 1979) and 'cognitive behaviourism' (Ledwidge 1978), and is characteristic of more liberal empiricist conceptions of psychological science. Thus Kimble (1989), for example, rejects the 'strict and restrictive' operational definitions of behaviourists, arguing that most theoretical concepts are 'open' to further definitional development and therefore serve a useful scientific role.

Despite the current popularity of this account, it resolves none of the problems of its more rigid precursor. It does nothing to resolve the complaint about the vacuity and circularity of theoretical explanations. At any point in time, it is only the case that the meaning of theoretical propositions is not exhaustively defined in terms of empirical laws: they are 'open' to further interpretation. It is not the case that they are defined independently of empirical laws. Consequently the determinate content of any theory at any point in time is just the content of the empirical laws to which it brings 'conceptual integration'. The problem of how this could provide any illuminating explanation of empirical laws remains as acute as ever.

The idea that hypothetical constructs usefully serve to guide and direct scientific research is also a complete illusion. For in order for a theory to be able to generate novel empirical predictions, this account requires the creation of new operational definitions relating 'partially interpreted' or 'open' hypothetical constructs to novel empirical laws. However, at any point in time, the determinate content of such constructs is specified by operational definitions relating such constructs to previously established empirical laws. On this account then, *the only guide to the discovery and prediction of novel empirical laws is our knowledge of previously established empirical laws*. However, if this is the case, then Skinner is quite correct to dismiss the logical apparatus of hypothetical constructs and operational definitions as redundant with respect to scientific development. Psychological science could develop just as well (or badly) by simply focusing on previously established empirical laws.

There are other problems concerning the operational definition of theoretical descriptions. Psychologists regularly claim that operational definitions are required to avoid the vagueness of our lay descriptions of psychological states. Although our lay descriptions of psychological states may be vague, it does not follow that the only route to their clarification is by operational definition in terms of observables. They may for example be clarified by stricter definitions in terms of their (intensional) contents and (intentional) objects.

Psychologists also regularly claim that theoretical descriptions of psychological states can only be empirically tested if they are given operational definitions in terms of observables. This is utterly false. Any contentful theory, in conjunction with causal hypotheses and auxiliary assumptions, can generate empirically-testable predictions. There is simply no good reason why the contents of psychological theories should be narrowly restricted to the contents of operational definitions. This restrictive doctrine promotes neither linguistic nor epistemic objectivity: it promotes only theoretical sterility.

Some psychologists might object that operational definitions are employed in psychological science not to provide general definitions of general theoretical descriptions but to provide specific definitions of the specific theoretical descriptions employed in individual experiments and empirical studies, in terms of the operations employed to evaluate the truth or falsity of a theoretical description with respect to such experiments and empirical studies. However, this riposte resolves no problems and creates its own.

This account is in fact very close to Bridgeman's original conception of the role of operational definitions. Bridgeman (1927:5) claimed of any theoretical concept that 'the concept is synonymous with the corresponding set of operations'. If this really is the case, then theoretical descriptions of mass, velocity, distance, electron orbit, and the structure of DNA would have different meanings when employed with reference to different empirical studies employing different empirical measures of these phenomena: that is, employing different operational definitions of these theoretical descriptions. Thus theoretical descriptions of the atom would have one meaning in experiments employing X-ray diffraction, and a quite different meaning in experiments employing spectrography. This would preclude the integration of theoretical knowledge concerning the atom gleaned from the first set of experiments with theoretical knowledge concerning the atom gleaned from the second.

Analogously, if theoretical descriptions of memory, emotion, attitude change, aggression, and intelligence are operationally defined in terms of the different empirical measures employed in different experiments, the terms 'memory', 'emotion', 'attitude change', 'aggression', and 'intelligence' would have quite distinct meanings with respect to these different experiments. This precludes the theoretical integration of knowledge gleaned about memory, emotion, attitude change, aggression, and intelligence from these experiments (including the recognition that the results of one experiment contradict the results of another, when they employ different operational measures).

Of course it is entirely proper for scientists to describe in experimental reports the empirical means employed to evaluate theoretical claims about memory, emotion, attitude change, aggression and intelligence, and their theoretical reasons for employing these empirical measures. However, this is quite different from defining the meaning of theoretical descriptions in these terms. The theoretical integration and comparison of knowledge gleaned about memory, emotion, attitude change, aggression, and intelligence requires that researchers provide an account of the content of theoretical descriptions of such phenomena that is logically independent of the particular empirical measures of these phenomena employed in particular experiments. The regular failure to provide such an account, and the regular commitment to the debilitating doctrine of operational definition, perhaps explains why it is so hard to provide a theoretical integration of the results of many experiments in social psychological science.

Relativism

Contemporary philosophy of science has been strongly critical of many of the details of the scientific empiricist account of science. Most of the recent critiques by Kuhn (1970), Lakatos (1970), Feyerabend (1975), and others are critical of the standard account of theory evaluation and of the classic distinction between theory and observation. However, the alternative accounts advanced by such theorists may properly be characterized as neo-empiricist accounts, since they essentially preserve the traditional instrumentalist account of theory as a set of intellectual constructions employed to bring conceptual unity to a set of empirical laws via the employment of correspondence rules and other auxiliary hypotheses. That is, they maintain the denial of the linguistic objectivity of theoretical descriptions.

According to the standard empiricist account of theory evaluation, competing theoretical systems are confirmed or falsified by reference to observational evidence. Since different theoretical systems can deductively accommodate the same range of empirical laws, the ideal way to select the best theory is via a *crucial experiment*, by the creation of an observational system concerning which the rival theories predict different things.

Thus for example the laws of refraction, reflection, and the rectilinear propagation of light were deductive consequences of Newton's corpuscularian theory of light and Huygens's rival wave theory of light. However, Newton's theory also predicted that light travels faster in a denser medium, and Huygens's theory predicted precisely the opposite. In 1850 Foucault measured the velocity of light in air and water using an interferometer and the result bore out Huygens's prediction but not Newton's. Given the invalidity of the sequent T → P, P ∴ T (where 'T' is a theory and 'P' a prediction, and '→' represents the conditional form 'if ... then ...'), this result did not conclusively establish Huygens's theory. However, given the validity of the sequent T → P, – P ∴ – T (where '– P' is the denial of a prediction), it may be held to have conclusively falsified Newton's theory. The idea that scientific theories can be effectively falsified is of course central to the Popperian account of science (Popper 1959).

This epistemically objective account of theory evaluation has been threatened by two related forms of criticism. In the first place, it is argued that theories are never tested in isolation, but always in conjunction with a 'network' of 'auxiliary hypotheses'. According to the *Quine–Duhem thesis* (Duhem 1906: 87; Quine 1953: 43), it is always possible to protect any scientific theory from falsification by the modification or replacement of auxiliary hypotheses employed in the derivation of a falsified prediction. The originally recalcitrant result can always be accommodated by derivation from the theory in conjunction with modified or alternative auxiliary hypotheses. Thus, for example, Newtonians did not reject Newton's theory of gravitation when faced with the anomalous orbit of Uranus. Rather, by modifying an auxiliary hypothesis about the number of the planets, they accommodated the orbit of Uranus and successfully predicted the existence of the planet now known as Neptune.

According to such accounts, scientific theories form a 'web of belief' (Quine and Ullian 1970), with 'paradigms' (Kuhn 1970) or 'hard cores' of 'research programmes' (Lakatos 1970) at the centre of the web. They are insulated from direct falsification by a 'protective belt' of auxiliary hypotheses that link the theory with observational descriptions at the 'periphery' of the web, since these auxiliary hypotheses can be modified or replaced to deal with any observational 'anomalies'. This poses a threat to the epistemic objectivity of theory evaluation by casting doubt upon the possibility of a crucial experiment to determine between rival theories that share a large measure of observational support. For it is claimed of any theory T_1 faced with a result that apparently falsifies T_1 but supports its rival T_2, that it can preserve evidential parity with T_2 by modifying auxiliary hypotheses to accommodate the anomalous result.

The epistemic objectivity of theory evaluation is also threatened by recent claims about the 'theory-informity' of observations. This doctrine appears to preclude the possibility of a crucial experiment by denying the possibility of 'theoretically-neutral' observational data. It denies the traditional distinction between the 'theoretical' and 'observational' levels of science. According to this account 'theoretical construction' is involved at even the most basic level of observation. It is argued that what a scientist observes is dependent upon his prior theories and expectations, and that in consequence scientists committed to different theories will make different observations (Feyerabend 1975; Hanson 1958; Kuhn 1970). Thus, just as one person may see a duck and another person may see a rabbit in the familiar gestalt duck–rabbit figure, according to their interpretation of the figure, so also two different scientists with different theories will observe different things when faced with the same evidence. Thus Brahe (a defender of the geocentric theory) facing east at dawn would see that the sun is rising against a fixed horizon, but Kepler (a defender of the heliocentric theory) would see that the horizon is rolling beneath a stationary sun (Hanson 1958). What one sees is held to depend upon what one *sees it as*, and what one sees it as is held to depend upon one's prior theories.

Now this doctrine is not so much a denial of empiricism as a return to the original idealist phenomenalism of Berkeley and Hume. According to classical empiricism and logical positivism, concepts of physical reality are 'logical constructions' that organize the raw material of perception. There is, however, one important difference. For whereas the older empiricism simply presumed that different individuals would employ the same intellectual constructions, in recent accounts there is no such presumption. On the contrary, it is argued that theorists raised in and committed to different scientific traditions and theories make different observations – in the same stimulus situations – informed by different theories. According to Kuhn (1970), they may properly be said to inhabit 'different worlds'. In consequence there can be no crucial experiments since competing theorists are bound to interpret the same result differentially according to their competing theories. In this essentially *relativist* account of theory evaluation, competing theories are said to be 'incompatible' but observationally 'incommensurable'. Since it is argued that no epistemically objective account of theory evaluation can in principle be provided by reference to the traditionally avowed logic of observational evidence, the only alternative appears to be sociological and psychological accounts in terms of dominant ideologies and powerful personalities (Barnes 1977; Bloor 1976; Feyerband 1975).

Social constructionism

Despite appearances, the recent *social constructionist* account of knowledge, including social psychological knowledge, is not so much opposed to the traditional empiricist account as a natural neo-empiricist and relativist development of it. Gergen (1982, 1985), for example, employs both the Quine–Duhem thesis and the doctrine of the 'theory-informity' of observation to support his claim that psychological theories are radically 'underdetermined' by observational data. These considerations lead him to make the explicit relativist claim that: 'Virtually any experiment used as support for a given theory may be used to support any alternative theory' (Gergen 1982: 72). He also dismisses the possibility of a crucial experiment by arguing that competing theories such as 'cognitive dissonance' and 'self-perception' theory are incompatible but incommensurable, citing the differential interpretations of classic experiments (concerning attitude-change) as support.

Much of the social constructionist argument is based upon such denials of the epistemic objectivity of theory evaluation. It has already been noted that this question is logically distinct from the issue of the linguistic objectivity of theoretical descriptions: denials of the epistemological objectivity of theoretical descriptions do not entail denials of their linguistic objectivity. Social constructionists also make much of the inadequacy of accounts of the meaning of theoretical descriptions in terms of operational definitions. However, the inadequacy of this instrumental account of theoretical description does not itself entail the non-descriptive nature of theoretical descriptions, if (as shall be shortly suggested) such theoretical descriptions can be defined independently of empirical laws.

Social constructionists also frequently suggest that if theoretical descriptions cannot be ostensively defined in terms of direct observations of the phenomena to which they purport to refer, and if their meaning cannot be specified by operational definitions in terms of observables, then such linguistic devices cannot be descriptive, far less linguistically objective. If our theoretical descriptions 'of' atoms and motives are not abstractions from observations, then it is held that such linguistic devices are 'social constructions' that cannot be conceived as accurate or inaccurate descriptions of an independent reality. Social constructionism 'views discourse about the world not as a reflection or map of the world but as an artifact of communal exchange' (Gergen 1985: 266).

REALISM

The general philosophical thesis of realism is an *ontological* doctrine to the effect that objects in the physical, social, and psychological world exist independently of our concepts of them and theoretical discourse about them (Bhaskar 1975; Manicas and

Secord 1983). This general philosophical thesis is shared by both scientific realists and contemporary empiricists. Relativists and social constructionists frequently deny this thesis, or deny its intelligibility.

The fact that realists and contemporary empiricists share this ontological assumption accounts for the fact that scientific realism is often represented as a form of empiricism or neo-empiricism. However, this is a major error. Scientific realism maintains the linguistic objectivity of scientific theories that empiricism denies. It is directly opposed to instrumentalist accounts of scientific theory.

Theory and meaning

Scientific realism is essentially a *semantic* doctrine about the meaning of theoretical propositions. According to scientific realism, theoretical propositions are putative descriptions of the properties and relations of postulated entities (e.g. atoms and motives), and such propositions are true or false according to whether the postulated entities exist and have the properties and relations attributed to them. According to scientific realism, the semantics and truth conditions of theoretical descriptions are *independent* of the semantics and truth conditions of the descriptions of empirical correlations they are often employed to explain.[2] *The meaning of theoretical descriptions is not determined by correspondence rules or operational definitions.*

According to scientific realism, the meaning of theoretical descriptions is determined by the theoretical model. Such descriptions frequently ascribe to postulated entities some of the dimensions of already familiar phenomena (Campbell 1921; Harré 1970; Hesse 1976), and exploit the semantics of our familiar descriptions of them. Thus Bohr's theory of the atom involves the descriptive claim that elements are composed of atoms that have some of the properties of (and on a much smaller scale than) planetary systems: they are composed of discontinuous particles with a nucleus (of protons and neutrons) that maintains other particles in motion via attractive forces. The meaning of these claims is quite independent of the meaning of the empirical laws governing spectral emissions that the theory was introduced to explain. Bohr's theoretical descriptions of the atom are true if and only if atoms exist and have the properties ascribed to them by these descriptions. Such descriptions are linguistically objective quite independently of any empirical laws they may be employed to explain.

This explains why many persons can and do understand the meaning of the descriptive claims of Bohr's theory (they understand, via the theoretical model, what it claims and what has to be the case for it to be true) although they have no inkling of the spectral emission laws the theory was introduced to explain. Analogously, many people understand the descriptive claims of Freud's theory of the unconscious but have little knowledge of the empirical phenomena (hysterical conversions etc.) it was introduced to explain.

This also accounts for the fact that most theories can furnish a non-vacuous explanation of empirical laws, since they embody semantic content additional to and independent of empirical laws. They embody information about systems additional to the correlational information contained in empirical laws, concerning dimensions and properties that underlie the causal regularities described by such laws. Thus the kinetic theory of gases provides an independently meaningful account of the compositional dynamics of gas systems (in terms of molecules in random motion) that provides an illuminative explanation of the correlations of pressure, volume, and temperature described by the gas laws. Analogously the 'hopelessness' theory of depression (Abramson, Metalsky, and Alloy 1989) provides an independently meaningful account of the content of agent representations that provides an illuminating explanation of many dysfunctional behaviours.

It also explains how theories can be semantically developed to generate novel predictions, via the development of the theoretical model. Thus Bohr's theory was developed (in the Bohr–Sommerfeld theory) by supposing that electrons are further analogous to planets insofar as they also rotate on their axes while traversing elliptical orbits ('electron spin'). This enabled the theory to explain the Zeeman effect and predict more complex spectral emissions. This is also familiar enough in social psychological science. Human psychological functioning or social interaction is theoretically described in terms of some of the properties of familiar systems, such as ball-bearings falling through Y-shaped pipes (Broadbent 1957), digital computers (Newell, Shaw, and Simon 1958), rule-governed games (Berne 1970), or the scripted performances of the theatre (Goffman 1959). Theories are developed by asking whether human psychological functioning and social interaction are analogous in additional respects to the familiar systems that provide the source of the theoretical model.[3]

This general account applies equally to the semantics of our everyday and developed scientific descriptions of psychological states. Theoretical descriptions of psychological phenomena such as beliefs and emotions are modelled upon some of the properties of linguistic utterances. Linguistic utterances have a *sense* (a meaningful or semantic content) and a *reference* (they are about some particular or class of particulars). In ascribing psychological states to ourselves or others, we ascribe states with *intensional* (meaningful or semantic) contents related to *intentional* objects (the objects to which our psychological states are directed). Thus for example in ascribing to myself the belief that the Eiffel Tower is in Paris I mean that I represent the Eiffel Tower (the intentional object of my belief) as located in Paris (the intensional content of my belief). In ascribing shame to another, I meant that she represents her action (the intentional object of her shame) as personally degrading and humiliating (the intensional content of her shame). Such descriptions are true or accurate if and only if the person represents a particular aspect of reality in the contentful way we ascribe to them. Such descriptions are linguistically objective quite independently of any empirical laws or phenomena such descriptions may be employed to explain. This is not to deny that references to psychological states can be employed to furnish causal explanations of human actions. Of course they can be and often are when we make *additional claims* about the causal role of psychological states in the generation of action. It is simply to stress that the semantics of psychological descriptions are logically independent of any causal explanations that references to psychological states may be employed to furnish. This is surely how we would wish it to be, since we want to preserve the theoretical possibility that a psychological state is present but does not play any role in the causal generation of an action. Thus a man may accurately ascribe to himself the belief that his child deserves punishment for a represented offence, but may inaccurately claim that this provides an adequate causal explanation of his violent actions. His actions may, for example, be best explained in terms of the unconscious emotions of psychoanalytic theory, or in terms of the presence of precipitating 'violent stimuli' (Berkowitz and LePage 1967).

Functionalism

The above-mentioned realist account of the semantics of theoretical psychological descriptions must be carefully distinguished from *functionalist* accounts of the semantics of such descriptions. These accounts treat psychological descriptions as causally defined in terms of postulated internal states that 'intervene' between observable environmental stimuli and behaviour. According to Lewis (1972: 112), the semantics of our theoretical psychological descriptions are determined by sets of causal propositions relating 'mental states, sensory stimuli, and motor responses'. Psychological states are defined generally as states 'apt for bringing about a certain sort of behaviour' (Armstrong 1968).

In this respect such accounts may also be said to advance a realist account of the semantics of psychological descriptions: they treat such theoretical propositions as putative descriptions of psychological states, rather than instrumental redescriptions of empirical laws. In another respect they may not be said to advance a realist account, since their account of the semantics of psychological descriptions is not independent of the empirical laws (relating stimuli and responses) that references to such psychological states are employed to explain.

The problem with such accounts is that they retain all the vices of traditional instrumentalist accounts and attain none of the virtues of a properly realist account. Since psychological states are defined in terms of their behavioural effects, references to such states cannot provide illuminating causal explanations of actions. My explanation of another's aggressive action in terms of his motive of revenge is illuminating because it ascribes to the agent a socially meaningful representation of his action (as a restitution of some prior injury) that plays a causal role in the generation of his aggressive action. I do not merely advance the vacuous truism that the type of psychological state that causes aggressive actions caused this one. Nor is it easy to see how the causally defined semantics of such theoretical psychological ascriptions could be developed to generate novel predictions.

This is not to deny that entities in social psychological and natural science are often ascribed causal roles. It is to deny that these ascriptions regularly play a role in the determination of the semantics of our descriptions of them. The semantic contents of most theoretical descriptions in natural science involve the ascription of composition and structure. The semantic contents of most descriptions of psychological states involve the ascription of contentful representations. The employment of such descriptions requires the addition of auxiliary causal hypotheses in order to generate causal-explanatory claims.

Neither is it to deny that entities are sometimes defined in terms of their causal role or properties. 'Gene' was originally defined as the entity whose transmission is responsible for heredity and variation; water is defined in lay terms as a clear liquid that can quench thirst, boils when heated, and freezes in cold weather, etc. It is to deny that references to theoretical entities defined in this way can provide illuminating causal explanations. An explanation of heredity and variation in terms of genes, where 'gene' is defined as the entity whose transmission is responsible for heredity and variation, is entirely vacuous. An explanation of heredity and variation in terms of genes, where 'gene' is independently defined in terms of the composition and structure of DNA, provides real illumination. An explanation of the properties of water by reference to the fact that it is water is wholly vacuous when 'water' is defined as any entity having these properties. An explanation of the properties of water by reference to the fact that it is water provides an illuminating explanation of these properties when 'water' is defined in terms of the molecular composition and structure of water.[4]

It is not a necessary condition of understanding the meaning of a theoretical description that one has knowledge of the causal or functional role of the entity referenced by the description. We can (and do) understand the meaning of theoretical descriptions of phenomena such as 'golgi bodies' or 'myelin sheaths', even though we have at present little inkling of their causal role. I may understand the meaning of theoretical descriptions of psychological states such as 'anger', and may correctly ascribe anger to a visitor from another culture (even as a lucky guess), although I may have no inkling how persons in that other culture respond to anger. I may understand the meaning of theoretical descriptions of psychological states such as 'shame', and may correctly ascribe them to myself long before I decide how to respond to them. I may understand the meaning of theoretical descriptions such as 'grief', but I may have to ask a psychiatrist how individuals are likely to respond to grief if I want to help a bereaved friend to whom I correctly ascribe grief.

Many suppose that the semantics of theoretical descriptions must be learned via their introduction within a network of causal explanatory propositions. There is no good reason to suppose that this is the case. The semantics of our descriptions of the elements documented by the periodic table of the elements can be and are frequently introduced by direct reference to the atomic composition and structure of these elements (in terms of which they are actually defined). Once we have grasped the semantics of these descriptions, we can then learn how the atomic composition and structure of elements referenced by such descriptions is causally implicated in the explanation of their diverse properties.

It is often said that we come to grasp the semantics of theoretical psychological descriptions – at our mother's knees – by their introduction within a system of causal-explanatory propositions (Churchland 1979). In fact this does not appear to be the case. Although of course as children and adults we frequently do reference psychological states in causal explanations of our own and other's actions, this does not appear to be a necessary developmental condition of our grasp of their semantics. By about age 2–3 most children have an extensive psychological vocabulary that enables them to attribute contentful psychological states to themselves and others (Olson and Astington 1986). However, it is not until age 4 that most children grasp the causal-explanatory employment of such descriptions:

> Very young children can take a causal view of the world. As far as the behaviour of people is concerned, they include as possible causes of behaviour only concrete objects and events. Independently of this causal view, these children can also formulate representations of mental states. This power develops in parallel with the causal view.
>
> Around four years of age, these two independent capacities come together; children enlarge their notion of 'possible causes of behaviour' to include mental states. From this point, mental states can be treated as both *causes* of behaviour and *effects* of perceptual exposure to a situation.
>
> (Leslie 1988: 37–48)

One reason why many philosophers may be tempted by the functional account is because of the traditional philosophical obsession with simple sensations such as pain. Given the familiar arguments advanced by Wittgenstein (1953) against the possibility of fixing the meaning of sensation descriptions by reference to a private inner ostensive definition, we seem obliged to characterize the semantic content of pain ascriptions in terms of their common environmental antecedents and behavioural expression: in terms of internal states caused by familiar stimuli (electric shocks, nails in our feet, etc.) which in turn cause familiar behaviours (yelling, grimacing, etc.).[5] This is because it is hard to explicate the socially meaningful content of such ascriptions in any other way. Given traditional empiricist assumptions about the homogeneity of sensation and cognition, it is natural for many theorists to generalize this account of the semantics of sensation descriptions to cover the semantics of our descriptions of psychological states such as beliefs, emotions, motives, etc.

This is unjustified, however, because there is simply not a parallel problem in the case of our descriptions of psychological states. There is no need to attempt to specify the semantics of such descriptions by either an 'inner' ostensive definition or causal story. Since our psychological descriptions are linguistically modelled, we already have all the semantic resources we require for psychological description when we have mastered the semantics of the names and predicates (and operators) of whatever language we use to describe and characterize the world. When we have grasped the semantics of descriptions such as 'the tree is tall' and 'my action was personally degrading and humiliating' we can ascribe these directed representational contents to ourselves and others: we can ascribe belief and shame to ourselves and others.

Testability and meaning

To make these claims is not to deny or neglect the important requirement that theoretical descriptions be testable by reference to observations. It is rather to stress that it is not a necessary condition of the satisfaction of this requirement that observational predictions are *directly* deducible from theoretical descriptions by virtue of an operational definition. Any independently meaningful theoretical description, in conjunction with causal hypotheses and other auxiliary assumptions, can generate testable predictions about observables. There is simply no reason to suppose that the contents of such theories must be restricted to the contents of operational definitions, or that testable predictions must be entailed by theoretical descriptions alone. The spectral emission laws do not define the content of Bohr's theory, and cannot be derived from Bohr's description of the atom alone: a good deal of additional causal hypotheses and auxiliary assumptions are required.

It seems quite clear that cross-cultural psychologists can reidentify emotions such as anger and shame in different cultures (Triandis 1980). Yet it is also clear that persons in different cultures are often angered by, or ashamed of, quite different forms of action (they recognize different forms of action as offensive and humiliating), and conform to quite different 'display rules' with respect to the behavioural expression of these emotions (Harris 1989). In consequence predictions about human action in any culture cannot be derived from descriptions of emotion alone, but must be derived from such descriptions in conjunction with auxiliary hypotheses about socially appropriate objects of emotion and display rules.

Social construction of theories

Social constructionists deny that theoretical descriptions in natural and social psychological science are linguistically objective: that they are true or false by virtue of independent facts about the natural or social psychological world. According to Gergen (1985: 266), for example, 'Social constructionism views discourse about the world not as a reflection or a map of the world but as an artifact of communal interchange'. The notion that theoretical propositions can provide accurate descriptions of an independent reality is dismissed as unintelligible, since it is held that there is no way of comparing reality with our descriptions or concepts of it (Wittgenstein 1969: 215; Kuhn 1970: 206).

For the realist, however, there is simply no reason to suppose that social constructionist denials of linguistic objectivity follow from social constructionist critiques of the standard empiricist account of theoretical meaning. The realist agrees that theoretical descriptions are frequently not 'reflections' of reality: that their semantics are not fixed by reference to ostensive or operational definitions that relate such descriptions to observable phenomena. The realist recognizes this (since the realist holds that the semantics of such descriptions are determined by the theoretical model) but consistently maintains that theoretical descriptions can be properly characterized as accurate or inaccurate.

The realist does *not* maintain that such descriptions are appropriately characterized as 'reflections' or 'maps' of reality. The realist does not postulate any mysterious relation of *resemblance* between our theoretical descriptions and the phenomena they purport to describe: the accuracy of a theoretical description is not held to be a function of its ability to 'picture', 'reflect', or 'copy' reality. This particular account of the accuracy of theoretical descriptions has its origin in traditional empiricist accounts of the nature of language and concepts: in terms of 'images' derived from 'sense-impressions'. It is uncritically adopted by the social constructionist as a (indefensible) criterion of accurate description. However, this doctrine forms no part of any realist account. For the realist the accuracy or inaccuracy of any description – 'theoretical' or 'observational' – is a function of the satisfaction or non-satisfaction of its truth conditions. The only means of determining this is by reference to the available empirical evidence.

The fact that scientific theories are themselves socially constructed is quite neutral with respect to the issue of linguistic objectivity. Many theoretical concepts and models are of course socially constructed or created, in the sense that their meaning is not defined ostensively or by operational definitions in terms of observables. The concept of the double-helical structure of DNA was not introduced by Watson and Crick to conventionally refer to something they could directly observe, but was socially constructed by them. This theoretical concept and its meaningful content were social in origin. Yet this does not preclude us from holding the view that Watson and Crick's theoretical account provides a more accurate description of the real dimensions of DNA than alternative theoretical accounts, nor does it oblige us to suppose that DNA itself – as opposed to our theoretical concept of it – is socially constructed or created.

The social constructionist claims that theoretical psychological discourse is performative rather than descriptive. In Chapter 2 it was noted that although theoretical psychological discourse undoubtedly can serve a performative function, this is entirely consistent with it also performing a descriptive function. An analogous riposte would apply to the social constructionist characterization of scientific knowledge as a form of social activity (Kuhn 1970; Gergen 1985). Some social activities, such as playing football or taking marriage vows, are clearly non-descriptive activities. However, other social activities, such as psychological theorizing, may be properly described as descriptive, since they have (socially defined) truth-conditions.

THEORY EVALUATION

One of the best introductions to 'cognitive psychology' is Lachman, Lachman, and Butterfield's (1979) book entitled *Cognitive Psychology and Information Processing*. About 500 pages of this book are devoted to the description of experiments and other empirical studies employed to assess a variety of theoretical claims about the mechanics of information processing. A philosophical and scientific realist would naturally conclude that the results of such experiments provide very good grounds for accepting some general theoretical descriptions of human information processing, since these provide the best and most plausible explanation of the outcomes of such experiments. Yet Lachman, Lachman, and Butterfield do not claim this. Their final chapter ends with the remarkable warning that it is too early to tell if human information processes are real or not!

That is, many scientific realists are also committed to *epistemic objectivity*: they believe we can have observational evidence for the accuracy or inaccuracy of theoretical descriptions, and rational grounds for supposing that one set of theoretical propositions provides a more accurate description of reality than other rival theories. It is of course true (as already noted) that questions about linguistic and epistemic objectivity are logically independent. It is quite possible to be a scientific realist and maintain the linguistic objectivity of theoretical descriptions, while at the same time accepting relativist denials of the epistemic objectivity of theory evaluation by reference to observations. One might consistently claim that Bohr's descriptions of the atom or psychoanalytic descriptions of unconscious psychological states are linguistically objective, while at the same time recognizing that it is enormously difficult (or impossible) to establish their accuracy. Nevertheless the realist is not forced to abandon epistemic objectivity because of the arguments developed by relativist philosophers of science that have been generalized by social constructionists (Gergen 1982) to the social psychological domain. For these arguments have considerably less force than is conventionally supposed.

Epistemic viability

According to the Quine–Duhem thesis, it is always possible to accommodate a failed prediction by modification or replacement of auxiliary hypotheses employed in the logical derivation of the prediction. As a general logical principle, this is of course correct: it is always logically possible to accommodate any particular result in this way. Whether this strategy is *epistemically viable* in any particular case is an entirely different question.

A theory may be said to be *epistemically viable* if it can continue to accommodate relevant observational data while preserving its original confirmation base. It is clear, however, that many modifications of auxiliary assumptions will *not* preserve the epistemic viability of a theory. If certain auxiliary hypotheses have been employed in the logical derivation of previous results that have supported the theory, then the modification or replacement of such hypotheses will result in the elimination or reduction of the original confirmation base: the original predictions will no longer be derivable. When competing theories that share the same confirmation base license different predictions in a novel domain, then it is rational to prefer the theory that makes the correct prediction if modifications cannot be made that preserve the epistemic viability of the competing theory (or theories). In such circumstances, although we perhaps cannot talk about logically conclusive observations, we can perhaps talk about epistemically decisive ones.

Of course there will be some cases in which it is possible to make modifications that can accommodate both the failed prediction and the original support for the theory. The point is that this is a contingent matter that depends upon the particular case. The preservation of the epistemic viability of a theory by such a strategy is not guaranteed *a priori* by any form of philosophical argument. There will no doubt also be cases where two (or more) competing theories will both (or all) remain epistemically viable in the face of the 'total evidence'. This is sometimes argued with respect to competing theories of space (van Fraassen 1980), and may be the case, for example, with respect to competing theories of memory search (Anderson 1981) and counter-attitudinal behaviour (Greenwald 1975). If this is a fact about these forms of theory, then it has to be faced (although it is much harder to establish the accuracy of these metatheoretical claims than the accuracy of particular theoretical ones, and many researchers retain a healthy scepticism). Yet no argument appears to demonstrate that this is inevitably or regularly the case with respect to competing theories.

Certainly the familiar claim that observations are 'theory-informed' does not. This claim has itself been the object of sustained criticism, on both psychological and philosophical grounds (Clark and Paivio 1989; Shapere 1964). It has been claimed that – in at least some cases – perception is not theoretically 'penetrable'. Thus the lines in the Müller–Lyer illusion still appear to be of different length even after we learn that it is an illusion and the theory that explains it (Fodor 1984). Nerve cells appeared in the same way under microscopes to lay and scientific observers throughout changes in theories of the nerve cell and the microscope (Hacking 1983).

Be that as it may, the 'theory-informity' of observations only poses a threat to the observational evaluation of scientific theories if the theories that inform the relevant observations are identical with (or entail) the theories that are the object of observational evaluation. While this may occasionally be the case (the possibility cannot be excluded *a priori*), it is palpably not invariably or regularly the case. The Watson–Crick theory of the double-helical structure of DNA was confirmed by the X-ray diffraction studies produced by Rosalind Franklin. These observations were informed by the theory of X-ray diffraction, not by Watson and Crick's theory of the structure of DNA. The theory of X-ray diffraction does not entail Watson and Crick's theory, nor any other rival structural theory (it only states how different structures will appear under X-ray diffraction). Analogously, experimental observations of humans attending or failing to attend apparently suffering victims may be theoretically informed by the assumption that such behaviours constitute instances of caring or apathy. Such theoretically informed observations do not, however, presuppose any theoretical causal explanation of the determinants of 'bystander apathy': they do not, for example, entail that the probability of intervention will decrease as the number of other bystanders present increases (Latané and Darley 1970).

Furthermore, since the theories that inform particular observations are also liable to inform a whole range of other observations in support of a theory, then we may doubt that recalcitrant observations can be easily given an alternative theoretical interpretation to protect a theory from falsification. For it is doubtful if such reinterpretations will preserve the epistemic viability of the evaluated theory. In the nineteenth century some defenders of Prout's theory – of the integral values of the atomic weights of elements – suggested dismissing the deviant fractional weight of chlorine as due to inadequacies of separation and purification techniques. However, most scientists recognized that the adoption of this strategy cast equal doubt upon the approximately integral values of the measured weights of other elements that provided the original support for Prout's theory, and dropped Prout's theory for that good reason (until the discovery of isotopes provided a partial solution of the anomaly). Analogously it would be difficult for a predominantly genetic account of intelligence differences to accommodate recalcitrant data that suggested a predominantly environmental account by casting doubt upon the adequacy of standard intelligence tests used to measure intelligence differences, for this would cast equal doubt upon any prior observations in favour of the genetic account that presupposed the adequacy of such tests.

Exploratory theories

The fact that theoretical descriptions are tied to observations not directly, but via networks of auxiliary hypotheses, tends to promote rather than undermine the epistemic objectivity of theory evaluation, for it enables us to demonstrate that at least some theories lack epistemic viability. The 'theory-informity' of observations also tends to promote rather than undermine epistemic objectivity, since observations critical in the evaluation of explanatory theories are not informed by those explanatory theories themselves, but by what may be termed *exploratory theories* concerning our modes of observational access to postulated theoretical entities. Thus the theory of X-ray diffraction stipulates how ultramicroscopic structures will appear under X-ray diffraction. It does not stipulate how the structure of DNA will appear under X-ray diffraction. Given a particular theory of the structure of DNA, the theory of X-ray diffraction can predict how DNA will appear if it has that particular structure. This *enables* us to test the theory of the structure of DNA: it enables scientists to *see that* DNA has a double-helical structure.

References to the ambiguous figures of gestalt psychology to illustrate claims about the 'theory-informity' of observation simply beg the question about the epistemic objectivity of theory evaluation. It is an essential characteristic of *ambiguous* line drawings such as the duck–rabbit figure that they do not contain sufficient information for the observer to determine whether the drawing depicts the head of a duck or rabbit. Consequently nobody can be said to *see that* it is a drawing of a duck or a rabbit; they can only be said to see it *as* the head of a duck or rabbit. Analogously, someone who sees a shadowed head in dim light cannot be said to *see that* it is the head of a duck or rabbit if there is insufficient visual information to make such an identification; they can only be said to see it *as* the head of a duck or rabbit. If they can visually discriminate a bob tail or hear a quack, then they can be said to *see that* it is a rabbit or *hear that* it is a duck. Contrary to standard relativist accounts (Brown 1977), *seeing as* is not a special case of *seeing that*: it is a case of *not being able to see that*. To claim that observation in science is analogous to observation of the ambiguous figures of gestalt psychology simply begs the question about the epistemic objectivity of theory evaluation by assuming that we never have sufficient grounds for preferring one theoretical description over another.

It might be objected that the epistemic viability of an explanatory theory faced with an anomaly can be preserved by employing a different exploratory theory. However, the general argument against the Quine–Duhem thesis applies equally on the level of exploratory theories. We simply cannot assume that alternative exploratory theories will be epistemically viable. We must also remember that exploratory theories are supported not only by their ability to theoretically accommodate a wide range of empirical data, but by their ability to conceptually support a variety of explanatory theories, without inconsistency or *ad hoc* adjustment. Thus the exploratory theory of X-ray diffraction provides conceptual support for explanatory theories that reference the structure of nucleic acids, the size of atoms, and many other compositional and structural properties. To abandon an exploratory theory to preserve a particular explanatory theory that is faced with an anomaly would not only regularly force the scientist to abandon the prior support (based upon the exploratory theory) for the particular explanatory theory faced with an anomaly. It would also regularly force the scientist to abandon the prior support (based upon the exploratory theory) for a whole range of other explanatory theories.

It must be stressed that all these points apply with equal force to social psychological science. At the very least, the social psychological scientist is epistemically no worse off than any other scientist who advances theoretical descriptions of 'unobservables'.

Any contentful theory, in conjunction with causal hypotheses and other auxiliary assumptions, can generate testable empirical predictions. These networks of causal hypotheses and auxiliary assumptions enable us to reject alternative theoretical descriptions that are not epistemically viable. Thus, for example, a number of competing theoretical psychological explanations of an individual's action may seem equally viable when the action is treated in isolation, but very few and perhaps only one may remain epistemically viable when the action is located within an established psychobiography (De Waele 1971). Moreover the social context of human action may give the social psychological scientist an epistemic advantage over the natural scientist by effectively precluding a wide range of alternative theoretical explanations:

> We tell a man who has driven his car over a curb, up a steep bank, thus running down the man who was blackmailing him, that his car was not out of control. Such cases lead us very readily to think of intentions as 'imbedded in human customs and situations' (Wittgenstein, *Investigations*, para 337).
>
> (Louch 1964: 112)

A sceptic might complain that theoretical social psychological science is epistemically disadvantaged because it lacks sense-extending instruments and exploratory theories, such as the electron microscope and the theory of X-ray diffraction. With respect to the first complaint that it lacks sense-extending instruments, it may be replied that it does not need them. Whatever problems we imagine we have about the observability of psychological states, they are not a consequence of their miniscule size or distant location (or low frequency etc.). With respect to the second complaint, that it lacks exploratory theories, it may be replied that it does not. It merely lacks confidence in them.

Observation

We may combine these points to cast serious doubt upon the common and cavalier empiricist assumption that psychological states cannot be observed. For it is far from obvious that this is in fact the case. The scientific empiricist defines the domain of the observable as those entities and their properties that can be determined 'by direct observation, and with good agreement among observers' (Hempel 1965: 127). If we take the criterion of intersubjective agreement in isolation, we can be said to see planets and nerve cells through telescopes and microscopes, and hear radioactive decay and the reef below via geiger counters and sonar soundings, if observers agree about what can be seen and heard. By this criterion we may be said to see trees and tables with our 'naked' eyes, and hear the pigeons in the attic and burglar in the basement with our 'naked' ears, if observers agree about what can be seen and heard. By this criterion, we may also be said to see her anguish and hear her pain, if observers agree about what can be seen and heard.

This puts the whole burden of the empiricist account of the observable upon the directness requirement. Yet none of the above supposedly-contrasting examples of seeing and hearing can be held to be direct in any epistemically significant sense. In none of these cases can perception be said to be direct in the sense that it is immune from error, and in fact this desideratum of foundationalist epistemology was abandoned long ago by scientific empiricists: they abandoned the certainty of the privately observable (sense-data) for the intersubjective agreement of the publicly observable. In none of these cases can perception be said to be direct in the sense that it is unmediated by theoretical interpretation. It is simply not true for example that our perception of trees and tables is unmediated by theoretical interpretation, any more than our perception of planets and anxiety.

In order to observe that there are trees or pigeons present, we need to employ intersubjectively-agreed exploratory theories about how trees and pigeons manifest themselves to our 'naked' eyes and ears. In order to observe that there are double-helical structures and observe that there is radioactivity in the vicinity of the factory, we need to employ intersubjectively-agreed theories about how such structures and emissions are revealed via X-ray diffraction photographs and geiger readings. In order to observe that actions are motivated by revenge or that agents are suffering identity crises we need intersubjectively-agreed theories about how such psychological states are expressed in human action and discourse.

Of course intersubjective agreement about these exploratory theories does not guarantee their accuracy or reliability. Nothing does. Their epistemic viability is always an open question. Their epistemic viability depends upon their ability to theoretically accommodate a wide range of empirical data, and their ability to conceptually support a variety of explanatory theories, without inconsistency or *ad hoc* modification. If this suggests that the epistemic warrant of explanatory and exploratory theories is given a circular justification by relations of mutual support, this is perhaps no bad thing. For it is hard to imagine any alternative form of justification.

Such an account will not of course satisfy those who would insist that our evaluation of scientific theories can only be characterized as epistemically objective if there is some way of comparing our theoretical descriptions with theoretically neutral observations of reality. Those who insist upon such a requirement will never be satisfied, for such a requirement is impossible to fulfil. Nevertheless, this account does enable us to characterize our theoretical judgements based upon our theory-informed observations as governed by the nature of reality, and not determined by psychological predilections, socio-political forces, etc. This is because it is ultimately the nature of natural and social psychological reality that determines the epistemological viability of our explanatory and exploratory theories.

Certainly, none of the relativist or social constructionist arguments canvassed in this chapter force us to conclude that it is impossible to achieve epistemic objectivity with respect to theory evaluation. Nor do any of these arguments force us to conclude that there is anything epistemically suspect about exploratory theories, or that exploratory theories in social psychological science are less reliable than those employed in natural science or everyday life.

This is not to deny that the theoretical judgements of some scientists may not be rationally based upon the available empirical evidence and may as a matter of fact be determined by psychological predilections, socio-political forces, etc. Nor indeed is it to deny that this may be the case with respect to the judgements of all scientists. This is an open empirical question (although a positive answer to it would undermine its own epistemic warrant). It is only to insist that no relativist or social constructionist argument establishes that this must be the case, by establishing that our theoretical judgements cannot be rationally governed by empirical evidence.

Scientific realism does not of course entail the epistemic viability of any theory (any more than it guarantees the epistemic objectivity of theory evaluation). The realist recognizes that the epistemic viability of any theory is ultimately an empirical question. It can only be answered by pressing particular theories to their explanatory and exploratory limits.

Nor of course does scientific realism entail the existence of psychological states or any other theoretical entities. There have been those who harbour ontological doubts about the reality of contentful psychological states. The scientific realist can recognize the legitimacy of such doubts, since the linguistic objectivity of our descriptions of such states entails that their truth or falsity is an open question. Thus sceptical critics from Watson (1924) to Stich (1983) do not doubt the linguistic objectivity of our descriptions of contentful psychological states. Rather they argue that as a matter of fact there are no contentful psychological states. The accuracy and epistemic viability of such claims is of course an entirely separate question, about which many (including the author) have serious doubts.

5

EXPERIMENTATION

LABORATORY EXPERIMENTS

Researchers have long recognized the difficulties of experiments employing human subjects. The laboratory experiment has been subject to more or less constant criticism for the past few decades, to the point where many writers have been led to talk of a 'crisis' in social psychological science (Elms 1975; Gergen 1978). Criticisms of traditional experiments have been made on moral, methodological, and philosophical grounds, although they have made little real impact upon the practice of the experimental analysis of human action. This is very likely because most critics who emphasize the meaningful nature of human action tend to deny the very appropriateness of experimentation, while those committed to a causal science feel that to abandon traditional forms of experimentation would be to abandon social psychological science.

The artificiality of experiments

The ubiquitous complaint about experiments concerns the 'artificiality' of studying human action in laboratory settings. It is complained that regularities manifested in such restricted and unnatural settings are not manifested in 'real life' or natural settings, and that consequently such studies have little or no explanatory relevance to real-life situations.

Now this may in fact be the case, although not for the usual reasons. The adequacy of laboratory experiments and causal explanations supported by them is not threatened by the fact that regularities manifested in the closed systems of laboratory experiments are not manifested in the open systems of the real world. Causal knowledge gleaned from such experiments can be employed to provide explanations of human actions in open systems. Thus, for example, if it can be established by experimental closure that aggressive actions are determined or influenced by 'violent stimuli', then instances of aggressive actions in open systems can be explained by reference to antecedent exposure to 'violent stimuli'. Such experiments do not license predictions about the regular correlation of 'violent stimuli' and aggressive actions in open systems, since in open systems this liability can be interfered with by social inhibition. To suppose otherwise is to confuse the logic of *causal-explanatory* enquiries with the quite different logic of *descriptive correlative* enquiries (see Chapter 3, pp. 67–9).

Internal and external validity

Unfortunately this confusion is regularly made in the social psychological literature, particularly with respect to the common distinction between the *internal validity* and the *external validity* of experiments (Campbell and Stanley 1966). Laboratory experiments are held to maximize on internal validity: the isolation and control of the experiment enables the investigator to make accurate judgements about causality. Laboratory experiments are, however, held to be low on external validity: the artificiality of the laboratory experiment casts doubt upon any causal-explanatory inferences employed to explain actions in the real world. Laboratory experiments are often contrasted with field studies in naturalistic settings, which are held to be high on external validity since they deal with real-life settings, but low on internal validity because of the absence of isolation and control. Indeed it has come to be accepted almost as an experimental fact of life that internal and external validity are inversely related, insofar as success in one area tends to be inversely related to success in the other: 'The research decisions which increase internal validity often do so at the expense of external validity' (Conrad and Maul 1981: 17).

Yet this is just a mistake, based upon the common definition of 'external validity' or 'ecological validity' (Brunswick 1955) in terms of the ability to predict regularities in open systems, and upon the empiricist assumption that this ability is some measure of the adequacy of causal explanations. On the contrary, as is the case in natural science, the external validity of an experiment is *directly* proportional to its internal validity. The adequacy of causal-explanatory inferences to 'real-world' open systems is directly proportional to the adequacy of closed experiments that provide evidential support for such inferences.

Consider, for example, Milgram's (1974) experiments on 'destructive obedience'. If these experiments do demonstrate the power of some authorities to generate destructive obedience in others (the liabilities of some persons to obey such authorities when commanded to harm another), then reference to such authorities can be employed to provide causal explanations of real-world instances of destructive obedience when preceded by commands from authorities. Such a reference can be employed to explain the actions of the nurses in the Hofling *et al.* (1964) study, who obeyed the orders of doctors to administer quantities of a drug that exceeded maximum dosage levels, and perhaps the actions of concentration camp guards according to Arendt's (1964) 'banality of evil' hypothesis. The adequacy of such explanations entirely depends upon the adequacy of Milgram's experiments. If Milgram's studies failed to achieve experimental isolation of these variables, then such causal explanatory inferences are quite unsupported by his studies.

Consider the conclusion Milgram (1974: 188) drew from his experiments: 'Something far more dangerous is revealed; the capacity for man to abandon his humanity, indeed the inevitability that he does do, as he merges his unique personality into larger institutional structures'. There is in fact nothing inevitable about this at all. Milgram's experiments also demonstrate a variety of interferences. Many subjects refuse to obey, given moral support from peers, cues suggesting real danger, etc. However, the failure of Milgram's experiments to license predictions about such open-system regularities casts no doubt whatsoever upon the adequacy of the causal-explanatory inferences noted above, for these inferences are entirely dependent upon the success of causal isolation in the experiments. Conversely the possible success of some predictions about open-system regularities does not provide any evidential support for these explanatory inferences.

This is not to deny that attempts to achieve experimental isolation often do cast doubt upon the adequacy of explanatory inferences drawn from such experiments. What has to be stressed is that this is not an *intrinsic* or ineliminable feature of experimentation in any form of science. Problems about the external validity of experiments in social psychological science usually arise because attempts to maximize internal validity become counterproductive: they increase rather than decrease the causal ambiguity of the investigated system, or they cast serious doubt upon the *identity* of the phenomena generated in such systems.

Experimental artifacts

Researchers recognize a number of 'interaction paradoxes' associated with social psychological research that are not usually present in natural science, and which cast considerable doubt upon the internal validity of experiments. In the natural sciences, although the activity of the experimenter is often responsible for the creation of the closed system under analysis, for example a sample of Uranium 239, the activity of the experimenter plays no role in the generation of the experimental effect. Uranium 239 would emit beta particles and transmute to Neptunium whether the experimenter was there or not. However, the same cannot be so easily presumed in the case of laboratory experiments in social psychological science, for often the activity of the experimenter, and the interaction between the experimenter and her subjects, does often appear to influence the outcome of the experiment. Thus the age, sex, and expectancies of the experimenter often seem to influence the outcome of the experiment. Such 'experimenter bias' and 'experimenter expectancy' effects (Rosenthal 1976) are compounded by what Orne (1962) calls the 'demand characteristics' of many laboratory experiments: the fact that many experimental set-ups suggest to subjects what is expected of them in experiments. Subjects are also influenced by the 'evaluation apprehension' (Rosenberg 1969) engendered by taking part in a closely monitored experiment. These and other 'contaminating' variables, such as the regular employment of volunteer or student subjects, do appear to cast serious doubt upon the internal validity of traditional laboratory experiments: 'A necessary precondition of the experimental method is that the phenomenon being investigated should not be materially affected by the procedure used to investigate it.... No such assumption is possible, unfortunately, with human subjects' (Beloff 1973: 11).

Strictly speaking, this is incorrect. The activity of the experimenter in natural science does often influence the outcome of the experiment. However, this effect is usually minimal, readily identifiable, and easily compensated for. Thus, for example, the measurement of the temperature or pressure of a system may decrease the temperature or the pressure. However, it is not obvious that the 'interaction paradoxes' associated with experiments in social psychological science can be treated as minor technical problems of the same order. It is also worth noting that failures to replicate instances of such artifacts, and the possible non-universal nature of such artifacts, only exacerbates the original causal ambiguities noted by the critics.

The problems caused by such artifacts should not be underestimated. However, some of these problems are not really problems at all, such as the problems associated with the use of volunteers or student subjects. They only appear as problems when we conceive of the purpose of a laboratory experiment as creating an 'unbiased sample' for the purpose of open-system prediction, rather than a closed system for the purpose of causal explanatory inference. For, if a volunteer or student manifests a power or liability in a laboratory experiment, then variants of that experiment can be employed to discriminate the enabling, stimulus, and interference conditions for such powers and liabilities. A reference to these conditions can then be employed to explain the actions of non-volunteer and non-student persons in open systems who also have these powers and liabilities. The purpose of the laboratory experiment is not to predict the actions of non-volunteer and non-student agents in open systems on the basis of the actions of volunteers and students in closed systems.

Furthermore, a number of these problems are misconceived, and in consequence traditional attempts to alleviate them only exacerbate these and other problems. For attempts to alleviate these interactions by greater experimental control cast serious doubt upon the *identity* of the phenomena investigated in such experiments.

Experimental alteration

Perhaps the most serious problem for the experimental analysis of human action arises because the experimenter's attempt to isolate action systems may not only influence the outcome of the experiment, but may alter or transform the very nature of the system investigated: 'The very act of bringing a variable into the laboratory usually changes its nature' (Chapanis 1967: 558).

Now this problem arises because of the fundamental nature of human actions and social practices, originally noted in Chapter 1. Human actions and social practices are *socially constituted*: they are constituted as actions and practices by social relations and representations. Thus, for example, a trial by jury is constituted by its legitimizing relations to legal, judicial, and penal systems, and an employment interview is constituted by relations of authorization with respect to the organizational structure within which it is located. A behaviour is constituted as an act of obedience by the participant agent's representation of his behaviour as directed towards the injury of another; a behaviour is constituted as an act of dishonesty by the participant agent's representation of her behaviour as the removal or receipt of goods or services that rightly belong to another.

Yet consider the difficulties of reproducing the factors influencing the judgements of jurors in a murder trial in isolation from the social relations that constitute real trials as trials, including the representation by participants that such relational criteria are satisfied. The critical assumption of the logic of closed experiments and causal-explanatory inference to real-world open systems is that the phenomena isolated in the experiment *retain their identity* under such isolation. However, this assumption cannot be presumed to hold for human actions and social practices. Natural-scientific phenomena such as tin, acids, and uranium isotopes can be re-identified in both closed and open systems because they are logically *atomistic* in nature. Their identity is determined by their intrinsic composition and structure. Many actions and social practices do not retain their identity in isolation from real-world relational contexts, because they are logically *relational* in nature. Their identity is determined by their relations to phenomena extrinsic to them. Thus a sample of tin retains its identity as a sample of tin when it is isolated in experiments from other factors (such as a local magnetic field) that may confound our causal judgements. But many actions such as jury decisions and acts of aggression do not retain their identity when stripped of their constitutive social relational and representational dimensions.

This poses a particularly acute problem for the experimental analysis of human action. We need to isolate actions and practices in order to evaluate causal explanations, but our activity of isolation tends to alter or transform the very phenomena we are trying to investigate. This poses the most serious threat to the internal and (thus) the external validity of experiments. The radical ambiguity created by alteration precludes causal explanatory inference from closed to open systems, since it is not clear what kind of phenomenon has been generated in the laboratory experiment.

Thus, for example, if a laboratory experiment does not reproduce the normal relations and representations of an employment interview, or introduces novel relations and representations (via contamination), it cannot be presumed to reproduce a laboratory analogue of an employment interview. Consequently it cannot provide support for any theoretical causal explanation of the social dynamics of employment interviews. If the behaviour of children striking dolls in laboratory experiments should be identified as 'play' rather than 'aggression' (given the peculiar context), then such experiments cannot be employed to provide empirical support for explanations of 'aggression' in young children (Secord 1983).

We can anticipate special problems with respect to the laboratory reproduction of participant agent representations of behaviour that are constitutive of actions such as aggression and dishonesty, given the isolation from real-world relational contexts and the special relational context of the laboratory experiment. Thus, for example, it is most doubtful if subjects represent their behaviour as directed towards the injury of others in traditional 'aggression' experiments. The absence of significant others (friends, colleagues, family, etc.) may not only remove a form of social inhibition, but may prevent the agent from representing his action as potentially injurious to another. It is particularly unlikely that subjects represent their behaviour in this way when experimenters provide a theoretical rationale and justification based upon learning theory for behaviours such as the infliction of electric shocks on others (Kane, Joseph, and Tedeschi 1976). In such experiments subjects may frequently represent their behaviours as *beneficial* to others (Baron and Eggleston 1972). If this is the case, then instances of aggression are not reproduced in such experiments, and such experiments cannot be employed to support causal explanations of instances of aggression in 'real-world' open systems.

Milgram also moves rather too quickly from the reasonable assumption that his subjects followed orders from an authority to inflict *painful* electric shocks to the rather more dubious conclusion that they followed orders to inflict *harmful* electric shocks. There is little doubt that subjects represented the experimenter as a competent authority, for in this (somewhat unusual) example the laboratory experiment was itself an instance of the form of authoritarian system investigated, in which subjects adopt an attitude of subordinating trust in another recognized as a competent authority in his field (as in a doctor–patient or scientist–technician relationship). Yet, precisely because subjects probably did adopt an attitude of subordinating trust in the experimenter, it is most unlikely that subjects would have represented their behaviour as harmful to the other subject. Rather they may have trusted that a competent experimenter would not allow anything potentially injurious to take place in a psychology experiment (Baumrind 1964). Indeed Milgram's experimenter constantly emphasized that, although the shocks were painful, they were *not* harmful. If this was in fact the case, then Milgram's experiments did not create instances of *destructive* obedience, and cannot be employed to support explanations of destructive obedience (such as the actions of concentration camp guards) in 'real-world' open systems.

Ambiguity, artificiality, and identity

Researchers often complain about the ambiguity of the results of laboratory experiments in social psychological science. By this they usually mean the causal ambiguity engendered by the difficulties of achieving experimental isolation. These problems are real enough, but the above discussion suggests a much more serious form of ambiguity concerning the *identity* of the phenomena isolated in laboratory experiments, which of course only compounds the problem of causal ambiguity. These problems in turn are themselves often engendered by the ambiguity of the experimental context experienced by participating subjects.

Now many have complained that these problems have been overstated. Perhaps this is true, although it is perhaps also better to overstate rather than understate them. Furthermore most defenders of the status quo tend to ignore or gloss over the problems of alteration. Thus Mook (1983) and Berkowitz and Donnerstein (1982) correctly point out that the failure to predict regularities beyond the confines of the laboratory need not cast doubt upon the adequacy of causal explanations derived from laboratory experiments, but fail to recognize the alteration that may be generated by isolation.

Many theorists also object to the apparent distinction between the artificiality of the laboratory experiment and the reality of the real world outside the laboratory. It is protested that the laboratory is also part of the real world, and that the folk that populate it are real people. Of course this is true, but the critical distinction is not between the artificial and the real, but between the closed experimental and open systems of the real world, and the difficulties of preserving the identity of actions and practices under conditions of experimental closure.

It is also true that some 'real-world' social phenomena are ambiguous and artificial. When social phenomena are identified in open systems as ambiguous, such as some emergencies, then of course it is perfectly proper to reproduce this ambiguity in experimental investigations of human action in such circumstances. Yet this simply does not excuse the ambiguity of laboratory experiments concerned with the analysis of human actions in situations which are *not* ambiguous, nor does it justify the extension of explanations covering ambiguous situations to non-ambiguous ones. Thus Milgram's experiments may support explanations of the actions of the nurses in the Hofling *et al.* (1966) study, since for the nurses and Milgran's subjects it was far from clear whether their actions were liable to injure others, but cannot be presumed to explain the actions of concentration camp guards, for whom the injurious consequences of their actions were all too obvious. Although some social phenomena may be identified in open systems as artificial, such as some retirement speeches and some dinner parties, the dynamics of such phenomena can only be established if the constitutive relations and representations of such phenomena are successfully reproduced in isolative experiments. Yet there is, of course, no reason why these particular dimensions should be reproduced in all laboratory studies. Social ambiguity and artificiality are features of some social phenomena. They are not intrinsic virtues of the laboratory experiment in social psychological science.

It is also true that it is sometimes not the aim of the experimental scientist to reproduce phenomena identifiable in open systems (Henschel 1980). Both natural scientists and social psychological scientists intentionally create *novel* phenomena in experimental settings, such as transuranic elements and synthetic petrochemical compounds, or psychoactive drugs and novel work practices. This is an entirely legitimate enterprise, but it is palpably not the purpose of most experiments in social psychological science, which are designed to evaluate causal explanations of actions and social practices identifiable in open systems. Furthermore, such experimental artifacts are rarely constructed with only the laboratory in mind, and usually aim to have causal explanatory relevance for the possibilities of action in open systems. Thus, for example, the investigation of novel forms of trial by jury (in which the jury decides the sentence as well as the guilt or innocence of the accused) will only have explanatory relevance to the possibilities of action in open systems if the constitutive dimensions of trial by jury are reproduced in such experiments.

Finally it is no response to complain that variable subject representations of action and context are controlled variables in laboratory experiments, insofar as subjects are assigned randomly to experimental groups. For the object of methodological concern is not the possibility of confounding causal variables, but the *identity* of actions in experimental settings. In order for our causal-explanatory inferences from laboratory experiments to be supported, it is necessary to establish how the subjects represent their behaviours. To allow the inclusion of an indeterminate number of variable subject representations would be like including an indeterminate number of other metals (copper, lead, tin, etc.) in the controlled experimental analysis of the causal powers of a particular metal such as silver. It would make a disaster of the experiment.

This is not to deny that variable subject representations of their own and others' actions and social context are of interest in their own right, insofar as they may have causal-explanatory relevance. However, if explanations of actions and practices in terms of different agent representations are to be evaluated in experiments, then such representations must be standardized in different experimental groups, or discriminated within the same experimental group via agent accounts.

There is, however, no guarantee that such procedures will be successful in fulfilling their purpose, for the analysis of agent accounts may reveal a general failure to reproduce the kinds of social psychological phenomena putatively studied by the experimentalist. Furthermore, sensitivity to these issues does not by itself ensure their resolution. For one may be perfectly aware of the social relational and representational dimensions of phenomena such as employment interviews or trials by jury, but at a complete loss as how to reproduce such phenomena in isolative experiments, short of the full-blooded reproduction of real interviews and trials by jury.

This has led some to conclude that the laboratory experiment should be abandoned in favour of field experiments, or a comparative causal analysis of human actions in different natural contexts. At the end of the day this may in fact prove to be the only solution, if the increased isolation and control of the laboratory, which normally decreases the causal ambiguity of studies in open systems, does so only at the unacceptable cost of increasing ambiguity with respect to the identity of the phenomena created in laboratory experiments.

DECEPTION EXPERIMENTS

The traditional response to the 'interaction paradoxes' of the laboratory experiment is the deception experiment, in which a 'cover story' is provided to disguise the real point and purpose of the experiment. Thus, although Milgram's experiment was designed to investigate the degree of 'destructive obedience' that could be commanded by authorities, it was presented to subjects as a learning experiment.

Moral problems

The deception experiment has also come in for a lot of recent criticism. Unfortunately much of this criticism has been on moral rather than methodological grounds. Yet there are no moral problems essential to the deception experiment that are not also shared by any other form of experimentation. Objections based upon the deception of subjects *per se* can be avoided by forewarning subjects about the possibility of deception in particular experiments (Horowitz and Rothschild 1970), or experiments in general (Holmes and Bennett 1974). Objections based upon the very real anxiety and distress suffered by subjects in deception experiments concerned with aggression, reaction to danger, and dishonesty apply to any form of experimentation employed to investigate these phenomena.

Methodological problems.

The most serious objections to the deception experiment are in fact methodological. The main point of the deception experiment is to eliminate or alleviate contaminating artifactual variables (Miller 1972; Cooper 1976). However, this means that the experiment as described to subjects (the 'cover story') cannot be a real experiment at all, for this would be to introduce new, albeit different, contaminating variables. It is therefore hardly surprising that subjects in such experiments regularly represent the 'experiment' as pointless, unreal, and highly ambiguous (Jourard 1968; Harré and Secord 1972; Forward, Canter, and Kirsch 1976). Thus, for example, Milgram's subjects complained that 'This is crazy' and 'I don't see any sense to this'. The meaning of the experimental situation is underdetermined by the information available, and this tends to generate variable rather than the standardized forms of representation required in laboratory experiments.

Essentially the same point can be made by noting the outcome of an Asch-type experiment on conformity conducted by Horowitz and Rothschild (1970). In order to avoid the moral objections to deception *per se*, they employed a group of subjects who were forewarned that the real purpose of the experiment was being withheld from them, as well as a group of deceived subjects, and a group of subjects fully briefed about the real purpose of the experiment (to investigate conformity as a function of group pressure). Since the 'forewarned' and 'deceived' groups both exhibited levels of conformity that were significantly higher than those exhibited by the 'prebriefed' group, the authors concluded that the moral problems of deception can be avoided without sacrificing methodological rigour by the employment of the strategy of forewarning.

However, this study does nothing to suggest the methodological adequacy of the forewarning strategy. Rather it casts serious doubt upon the methodological adequacy of the deception experiment. For what this study demonstrates is that subjects who were explicitly informed that the experiment was ambiguous acted in the same fashion as those subjects who were supposed to be deceived. This strongly suggests that the experiment was as ambiguous for subjects in the deception group as it was for subjects in the forewarned group.

The fundamental problem with the deception experiment is that it is only designed to eliminate or alleviate contaminating variables. It completely ignores the problem of experimental alteration. In consequence deceptive strategies designed to camouflage the real point of the experiment exacerbate the problem of alteration by increasing the ambiguity of the experimental context.

EXPERIMENTAL SIMULATION

Intensional stimulation

Nevertheless the deception experiment has the right idea, for it attempts to create an *intensional simulation*. That is, it aims to reproduce and standardize constitutive subject representations without attempting to reproduce the normal relational context. Yet because it ignores the fact that such representations are often based upon discriminated features of the relational context, it is bound to fail.

The partial constitution of action by agent representations constitutes a potential advantage for the experimenter, if she can make a virtue out of this necessity. For it is sufficient for the purposes of experimental isolation and causal-explanatory inference that experiments are successful in reproducing the intensional contents of subject representations, for the constitutive nature of these contents will ensure the re-identifiability of actions in isolative experiments, and the explanatory relevance of such experiments to 'real life' open systems. Thus it is not in fact necessary to reproduce actual instances of dishonesty and aggression in laboratory experiments, or employment interviews and trials by jury. It is sufficient to reproduce the intensional contents of the representations that are constitutive of these actions and practices in open systems.

The deception experiment aims to achieve *intensional simulation* by deception. The simulation experiment aims for an *intentional* intensional simulation, by instructing subjects to act *as if* they represent context and behaviour in the experimentally desired fashion. In active simulation experiments participants are asked to act in accord with scripted representations that are possible representations of 'real-world' social contexts (Smith 1975). For example they are asked to represent the situation as if they were a candidate in an employment interview, as if they were a person asked to make a counter-attitudinal speech, as if they were a policeman about to arrest a black offender in a ghetto area, as if they represented a situation as a threat or an emergency, as if they were requested by an authority to harm another, as if they were a juror deciding the guilt or innocence of a defendant with a psychiatric history, etc. The essential feature of this form of simulation is that participants act as if they represented social reality according to the constitutive dimensions requested by the experimenter.

Simulation and 'role-playing'

Now this form of experimental simulation has often been classified as 'role-playing'. This is most unfortunate for a number of reasons. In the first place, it is often dismissed by association with a form of passive simulation, in which subjects predict what they would do in various scripted scenarios. This leads to the justified complaint that this form of experimentation only tells us 'what men think they would do. It does not tell us what men would actually do in the real situation' (Freedman 1969: 114). In order to determine what agents do, one has to employ *active* simulation, in which agents act in accord with scripted representations.

Second, it is not essential that subjects play any particular role in active simulation experiments. Although it is true that in some experimental situations subjects are asked to represent the situation as if they were a policeman, interviewee, or juror, at other times they are simply asked to act as if they represented a situation as an emergency or an opportunity for dishonesty. Simulations in which subjects are asked to adopt particular social roles are special examples of experimental simulation, not the general form of all experimental simulation.

Third, the term 'role-playing' suggests that a particular form of theatrical skill is required to take part in such experiments, and that participating in such experiments is a form of mere 'play-acting'. However, no special form of acting skill is required that involves a special ability to empathize with others. If participants in active simulations play the parts of anyone at all, they play the parts of themselves in specifically represented situations, or themselves in scripted roles with which they are familiar. This last requirement marks perhaps the only point relevant to effective simulation. All other things being equal, it would be better to employ those familiar with particular social roles (prison warder, social worker, teacher, etc.) rather than those who are not, when such matters are the object of study.

The accusation of mere 'play-acting' is perhaps the most damaging, and no doubt accounts for the greatest amount of hostility among researchers to the simulation experiment. Yet standard complaints about the lack of realism and involvement in experimental simulations are ill-founded. Many studies have attested to the degree of realism and involvement that can be achieved in simulation experiments. The simulated attack and defence of Grindstone Island (Olson and Christiansen 1966) and the Stanford prison study (Hanay, Banks, and Zimbardo 1973) had to be prematurely terminated because participants became *too involved* (to the point of danger to themselves and others). Mixon (1972) notes that subjects who participated in his simulation of Milgram's experiments exhibited the same 'spontaneous nervous and emotional behaviour' as Milgram's subjects.

Experimental construction

However, there is a much more fundamental error that undermines this complaint. It is frequently assumed that the simulation experiment, like any laboratory experiment, is designed to predict what agents will do in 'real-world' open systems. However, this is not the purpose of *any* experiment. The purpose of experiments in social psychological science is to determine the enabling, stimulus, and interference conditions for human powers and liabilities. Furthermore the purpose of simulation experiments *is not to simulate human actions. Only constitutive relations and representations are simulated, not human powers and liabilities themselves.* When human powers and liabilities are manifested in simulation experiments, then the conditions of such experiments can be varied to discriminate enabling, stimulus, and interference conditions.

This in fact constitutes the primary advantage of experimental simulation. It has the potential to achieve isolation without alteration. By progressively constructing and modifying scripts for simulation, one can discriminate the conditions that underlie the liabilities of policemen to become aggressive in the context of an arrest or the liabilities of social workers to ignore real indicators of child abuse, and the conditions that enable some teachers to be effective communicators and some citizens to resist and surmount pressures to conform. In this respect experimental simulation represents the closest analogue of experimentation in natural science, and the practice of constructing social contexts by simulation represents the closest parametric equivalent of experimental studies designed to discriminate generative and interference conditions.

Experimental evaluation

There have been many experimental evaluations of the utility of simulation experiments by reference to their ability to reproduce the outcomes of deception experiments (not surprisingly perhaps, the results have been very mixed (Miller 1972)). However, this strategy is fundamentally misguided.

In the first place, many of these experimental comparisons involve essentially passive forms of simulation employing subject predictions only. Second, they make the gratuitous assumption that deception is an effective experimental strategy, with the natural consequence that even when simulation experiments do reproduce the results of deception experiments, such experiments appear derivative and superfluous. Yet since the simulation experiment is introduced precisely because of justified methodological doubts about the success of deception experiments in achieving intensional simulation, there is no reason to adopt them as the standard of methodological adequacy for simulation experiments, and in fact no reason to expect subjects to act in the same way in simulation experiments. Suppose, for example, that we wish to investigate conditions that underlie the human liability to inflict real harm upon others given commands by authorities. We have noted that there is good reason to doubt that Milgram was successful in achieving the intensional simulation of representations of real harm in his experiments. Why then should we expect agents to act in the same way in simulation experiments that are successful in achieving the intensional simulation of representations of real harm?

There is, in any case, something peculiar about requiring an independent experimental validation for simulation experiments. Notice that no-one bothers to require this form of validation for the deception experiment itself, or for laboratory experimentation in general (for if we could provide such an independent empirical justification, experimentation would be itself superfluous). This is not to deny that useful work can be done on the evaluation of how intensional simulations can be most effectively created. For it should be noted that emotional involvement is no guarantee of successful intensional simulation. The 'spontaneous nervous and emotional behaviour' of subjects in the Milgram experiment – and Mixon's simulation of it – is no guarantee that subjects represented their behaviour as harmful to the victim, since the same form of behaviour can be observed in subjects who watch the video of the Milgram experiment (and who are perfectly aware of the deception). What is important in a simulation experiment is not emotional involvement but *intensional engagement*, and work certainly does need to be done on how this can be best achieved (e.g. use of real props, the employment of persons with experience of the social roles of warders and prisoners – rather than students – in prison studies etc.). For a useful beginning see Yardley (1982).

Powers and liabilities in simulation experiments

There can, however, be little serious doubt that human powers and liabilities can be investigated in simulation experiments. For part of what it means to attribute a persuasive power to another is that she can persuade others in simulated contexts. Part of what it means to attribute aggressive or dishonest liabilities to agents is that they will be – and cannot help being – aggressive and dishonest in effectively simulated stimulus contexts. A teacher who has the power to communicate effectively can manifest this power in a simulated context if she really has this power. The simulated context can be reconstructed in various ways to discriminate enabling and interference conditions. Someone who is liable to become aggressive in the presence of 'violent stimuli', or a social worker who is liable to ignore indicators of child abuse, will manifest this liability in experimental simulations if they really are subject to it. The simulated context may be reconstructed in various ways to discriminate means of surmounting this liability.

Many researchers who conceive of simulation experimentation as mere 'play-acting' fear that subjects will 'feign good' in simulation experiments because of 'evaluation apprehension'. Yet this fear is quite unwarranted, and belied by the common practice of employing simulation in personnel selection and evaluation. As Mixon (1980) notes, trainee police officers who dearly wish to present themselves as disciplined under stress will fire randomly into a crowd in simulations of a ghetto arrest. Analogously, many agents in real life want to present themselves in the best light, but betray their liabilities to be aggressive and dishonest to their prospective wives and store detectives.

In actual fact it is usually more difficult to surmount liabilities in these forms of simulation than in real life. For the characters simulated by policemen, social workers, and teachers in personnel evaluations are usually composites of the worst sort of characters they have come across in their years of accumulated experience. If trainee policemen, social workers, and teachers can deal with them in simulations, they can deal with anything in real life. Since significant human powers and liabilities are clearly manifested in such simulations, there is no reason why variants of the scripted simulation cannot be employed in experimental explorations of enabling, stimulus, and interference conditions.

This takes us finally to the complaint that even if the above defence of the simulation experiment is sound, this form of experimentation is still subject to the same forms of experimental contamination as traditional experiments. While this is true to some extent no doubt, it is also much exaggerated. It has already been noted that 'evaluation apprehension' presents no serious impediment to the investigation of human powers and liabilities. 'Experimenter expectancy' is also only a problem if we conceive of the laboratory experiment as designed to predict what agents will do in open systems (so that subjects may try to confirm or falsify the prediction). However, it is doubtful that this will present a problem in experiments designed to discriminate the enabling, stimulus, and interference conditions for demonstrated human powers and liabilities, and described as such to participants. For the participants in simulation experiments have a parallel interest in correctly discriminating such conditions, in order that they might extend their powers and surmount their liabilities.

Nor is it a viable objection to complain that the simulated context will have 'demand characteristics'. For *part of the point* of experimental simulation is precisely to determine what demands of the simulated context promote and impede forms of action. The experimenter wishes to identify, for example, the implicit rules and social expectations of the social contexts of trial by jury, marital disputes, and wage negotiations. This is the proper object of contemporary studies of the logic of 'situated action' (Ginsburg, Brenner, and von Cranach 1985). Demand characteristics are problematic only when they are the *wrong* demand characteristics, when the laboratory experiment creates demands that are quite different from the demands of the social system investigated but not successfully reproduced or simulated in the experiment.

Evaluation of psychotherapy

One way of illustrating some of these points is by noting the unique way in which the problem of alteration arises in the evaluation of psychotherapy. Eysenck (1952) claimed that the efficacy of any form of psychological therapy could only be demonstrated if it produced improvement or cure rates (for specific psychological disorders) superior to the improvement or cure rates produced by 'spontaneous remission': the improvement or cure rates of patients who received no psychological treatment. However, it was quickly recognized that the concept of a 'no-treatment' control group is a fiction, since evidence suggests that interviews by general practitioners, and sympathy and support received from spouses, friends, colleagues, priests, etc., can have a powerful therapeutic effect (Malan 1975). Thus recent experimental evaluations of psychological therapy have been concerned to demonstrate the superiority of the effects of professional[1] psychological therapy over such 'non-specific' effects, and have employed 'placebo' or 'pseudotherapy' treatments to control for those elements of professional psychological therapies not referenced in theoretical accounts of their efficacy, such as client expectancy and therapist commitment. There has been increasing recognition of the social psychological nature of such 'non-specific' effects (Strong 1978). Indeed it should be recognized that psychological therapy is an intrinsically social psychological phenomenon, since it is intentionally sought and practised by individuals in socially meaningful contexts. Frank (1974) has suggested that the feature common to all successful psychological therapies is the ability to interact with a trusted and respected person in a course of activities that both believe may produce a therapeutic change. This may be treated as an informal characterization of the *social constitution* of psychological therapy.

However, this characterization may also be transformed into a theoretical causal-explanatory claim: that the efficacy of all therapies may simply be a product of the interaction of the client with a trusted and respected person in activities that both believe may produce a therapeutic change. This may be treated as a theoretically sufficient explanation of the efficacy of any form of psychological therapy, be it psychoanalytic, behaviourist, cognitive, etc., or some combination thereof. This is the alternative explanatory theory that is supposed to be eliminated by employing control groups that include everything but the theoretically efficacious elements of the professional psychological therapy employed in the experimental group. If the improvement or cure rates in the experimental group are significantly superior to the improvement or cure rates in the control group, then we can conclude that the efficacy of the professional psychological treatment under investigation cannot be accounted for (or cannot be wholly accounted for) in terms of the social psychological dimensions common to all forms of psychological therapy. This provides empirical support for the theoretical account of the efficacy of the professional psychological treatment.

The problem arises in the following way. Most researchers conceive of 'non-specific' factors such as treatment credibility, client expectancy, and therapist commitment in terms of experimental contaminants: they are treated as instances of contaminating variables such as 'demand characteristics' and 'experimenter expectancy' (Bernstein and Nietzel 1977). However, in the social context of psychological therapy, factors such as credibility, expectancy, and commitment are not experimental contaminants: *they are constitutive features of the therapy session.*

In standard experiments in social psychological science, the experimenter's experimental goals are an *extrinsic* factor (i.e. not the object of experimental analysis) that may function as an experimental contaminant. In experimental evaluations of psychological therapy, the therapist's treatment goals are an *intrinsic* (constitutive) component of the therapy session. In standard experiments in social psychological science, subject expectations are *extrinsic* factors that may function as experimental contaminants. In experimental evaluations of psychological therapy, client expectations and perceptions of credibility of treatment are *intrinsic* (constitutive) components of the therapy session. Psychological therapy is not itself an attempt to achieve experimental isolation: it is an attempt to achieve therapeutic change. The constitutive components of psychological therapy – expectancy, credibility, commitment, etc. – must be reproduced in any control group to at least the same degree as they are present in the experimental professional treatment, if such groups are to serve as experimental controls for the social psychological factors common to all forms of therapy.

Unfortunately these factors are conventionally represented as experimental contaminants. The experimental design of most evaluations is negatively conceived: the aim is to ensure that the theoretically efficacious elements of the experimental professional treatment are eliminated from the control treatment. In consequence the social psychological dimensions constitutive of psychological therapy tend to be eliminated or attenuated in control groups. It is very doubtful if the 'control treatments' employed in control groups, such as mathematical puzzles and unstructured discussions, are as credible to clients as professional psychological therapies (Borkovec and Nau 1972). It is even more doubtful if therapists running control groups are as committed to the efficacy of the 'control treatment' as therapists running experimental groups are to the efficacy of professional psychological treatments. In fact therapists running them are often committed to the theoretical *non-efficacy* of such 'control treatments'. In extreme cases it may be said that these constitutive dimensions are eliminated or attenuated to such a degree that the 'control treatment' *is not any form of psychological treatment at all*: it is in this unique respect that the problem of experimental alteration arises in the experimental evaluation of psychological therapy. This casts serious doubt upon the methodological adequacy of many experimental evaluations of psychological therapy. The superior treatment outcomes of experimental professional treatments over 'control treatments' may be a simple function of the higher levels of expectancy, credibility, and commitment in the experimental professional treatments.

If control groups are to serve their purpose in eliminating a theoretical explanation of the efficacy of professional psychological therapies in terms of the social psychological dimensions common to all forms of psychological therapy, they must be conceived in a more positive fashion. They must be designed to ensure that the 'control treatments' employed are at least as credible to clients as the experimental treatments, and that therapists employing 'control treatments' are at least as committed to their efficacy as therapists employing experimental professional treatments.[2]

The general point may be stated in the following way. 'Demand characteristics' are problematic in standard experiments only when they are wrong demand characteristics: if they are peculiar to the artificial laboratory context, rather than naturally embedded in the social system putatively under investigation. In the case of the experimental evaluation of psychological therapy, it is not their artificial presence in experimental or control treatments that is the problem. It is rather that the normal demand characteristics of psychological therapy (that may promote therapeutic change) are absent from, or attenuated in, 'control treatment' groups.

6
ACCOUNTING

One potentially very powerful exploratory resource that can be employed in social psychological science is the ability of human agents to provide accounts of their psychological states. This resource has been historically neglected by researchers, and remains underdeveloped and underexploited. It is of course the case that like any exploratory theory, the epistemic viability of this resource can ultimately only be assessed by its ability to accommodate empirical data and conceptually support a variety of successful explanatory theories. Thus no attempt is made in this chapter to establish its epistemic viability. However, it is also true that it has never been given a theoretical chance to demonstrate its utility. In this chapter it is argued that there are simply no good reasons for its historical neglect. The reasons usually given for ignoring this exploratory resource are thoroughly bad ones.

A number of preliminary distinctions are perhaps in order to avoid some common misinterpretations of this claim. Agent accounts of their psychologies may be employed as heuristic devices that suggest possible causal explanations of social psychological phenomena. Thus subject 'protocols' are regularly employed in cognitive psychology to suggest hypotheses about cognitive processing that are then independently tested (Ericsson and Simon 1984). Post-experimental accounts of how agents represented what was going on in 'cognitive dissonance' experiments in social psychology have suggested alternative explanations that have been independently supported by further experiments, and which have refined our understanding of this social phenomenon (Secord 1990). As a heuristic device, agent accounts of their psychologies have regularly demonstrated their utility. This is not, however, the manner in which they are conceived as an exploratory resource.

Rather it is suggested that agent accounts of their psychologies enable us to *identify* their psychological states, in the manner in which our microscopes and 'naked' eyes enable us to identify nerve cells and trees.

It is not suggested that agents are epistemic authorities on the causal explanation of their actions or their modes of psychological processing. No doubt subjects regularly do err in advancing causal explanations of their actions (Nisbett and Wilson 1977) and logical reasoning processes (Johnson-Laird 1983). It is suggested that agents may very well be epistemic authorities with respect to their accounts of their psychological states, and that this is entirely consistent with a recognition of their lack of epistemic authority with respect to causal explanations of their actions and cognitive processes.

To suggest that agents may be epistemic authorities with respect to their psychological states is not to endorse or defend any form of 'introspection', 'self-perception', or 'cognitive monitoring'. On the contrary, the analysis of agent accounting is designed precisely to reject this ancient and popular conception of self-knowledge of psychological states.

SELF-KNOWLEDGE: INFERENCE AND PERCEPTION

Telling more than they can know

Philosophers and psychologists are not well known for their inter-subjective agreement concerning matters of the mind. However, the modern consensus of philosophers and psychologists is that agents' accounts of their psychological states are unreliable and regularly inaccurate.

For many years they disagreed. Since the demise of 'introspective psychology' in the early part of this century, psychologists have been highly sceptical of agent accounts of their psychological states, arguing that self-knowledge of psychological states is indirect and uncertain. For many years, indeed for a number of centuries, most philosophers argued that self-knowledge of psychological states is direct and as certain as any form of human knowledge can be. Recently, however, many philosophers have joined the psychologists, declaring self-knowledge of psychological states to be indirect and uncertain (Flanagan 1984; Stich 1983). The conventional wisdom is that empirical studies such as those documented by Nisbett and Wilson (1977) and Nisbett and Ross (1980) have demonstrated that self-knowledge of beliefs, emotions, motives, etc. is regularly inaccurate and thus unreliable as an exploratory resource. For example, in their paper entitled 'Telling more than we can know', Nisbett and Wilson (1977: 233) claim that: 'The accuracy of subjects is so poor as to suggest that any introspective access that may exist is not sufficient to produce generally correct or reliable reports'.

Some contemporary philosophers have not merely been content to endorse this conventional wisdom. Some, most notably Paul Churchland (1979), have claimed that self-knowledge of psychological states may be *universally false*. The conclusion is easily reached, via the joint assumptions that self-knowledge of psychological states such as emotions, beliefs, attitudes, etc. involves a form of 'theoretical inference' or 'theory-informed perception', and that the 'folk-psychological' explanatory theories that inform our inference and perception may be universally false.

Sensation and cognition

One of the ironies of the early disagreement between philosophers and psychologists is that both their accounts were based upon the traditional empiricist assumption about the *homogeneity* of sensation and cognition. In the classical empiricist account of cognition, our thoughts or 'ideas' were held to differ from sensations in degree but not in kind: they were held to be 'copies' or 'faint images' of 'sense-impressions'. Thus many philosophers argued that our self-knowledge of pain and sense-data is direct and certain, and then generalized this account to cover self-knowledge of psychological states such as emotions, motives, and beliefs. Many psychologists treated the failure of 'introspective psychology' – the experimental analysis of the 'elements' of perception – as demonstrating the unreliability of self-knowledge of sensory experience, and then generalized this scepticism to cover self-knowledge of psychological states.

We have already noted how this empiricist assumption about the homogeneity of sensation and cognition spawned the theoretically debilitating doctrine of meaning empiricism. Yet although this assumption has been abandoned by contemporary psychologists and philosophers, it still continues to inform the current debate about the status of self-knowledge. Most philosophers and psychologists conceive of self-knowledge of mental states[1] as a form of perception or experience of 'inner states'. However, although our self-knowledge of sensations such as pains (and experienced sense-data) may be readily conceived as a form of 'inner perception', the same cannot be said for self-knowledge of psychological states such as emotions and beliefs. Indeed self-knowledge of psychological states may best be characterized as externally or socially directed rather than internally or psychologically directed.

It is perhaps worth recalling at this stage the essential difference between sensations such as pain and cognitive or psychological states such as emotion and belief. According to contemporary accounts, sensation and cognition are different in kind. Psychological states such as emotions and beliefs have intensional contents and intentional objects. Sensations do not have intensional contents or intentional objects (although like psychological states and everything else, they do have causes). If I see another deep in thought, it makes sense to ask her what she is thinking of and what she is thinking about it. If I see another in extreme pain, it makes no sense at all to ask him what his pain is of or about (it does of course make sense to ask him where it is located, what caused it, etc.).

Introspective psychology

In support of their sceptical conclusion about self-knowledge, most psychologists and philosophers cite the failure of 'introspective psychology', and the experimental studies documented by Nisbett and Wilson (1977) and Nisbett and Ross (1980) that appear to demonstrate that self-knowledge is regularly inaccurate.[2]

However, the failure of 'introspective psychology' is simply irrelevant. The experimental studies conducted by Wundt and Titchener at the turn of the century were exclusively concerned with the introspection of the 'elements' of sensory experience. None of these studies was concerned with self-knowledge of intentional psychological states such as beliefs and emotions. The failure of introspecting subjects to reach agreement on accounts of their introspection of sensory elements has simply no bearing no the question of the abilities of agents to provide accounts of their intentional psychological states, if, as noted above, sensations and intentional psychological states are different in kind.

It is of course true that some of the studies of the 'Wurzberg

School' were avowedly concerned with 'thoughts'. Yet in these studies 'thoughts' were themselves conceived in terms of sensational images – hence the 'imageless thought' and other controversies that led to the demise of 'introspective psychology'. 'Imageless thoughts' only constitute a problem for those who mistakenly assume the homogeneity of sensation and cognition.

Self-knowledge as theoretical inference

With respect to the studies documented by Nisbett and Wilson and Nisbett and Ross, it should be noted that only *two* of the multiplicity of studies documented by these authors are concerned with self-knowledge of intentional psychological phenomena. These are Schachter's (1965) analysis of emotion and Bem's (1967) analysis of attitude avowals. Nisbett and Ross (1980: 227) claim that: 'Knowledge of one's emotions and attitudes, though believed by the layperson (and many philosophers) to be direct and certain, has been shown to be indirect and prone to serious error'. However, neither of these studies provides any support for the conclusion that subjects are ever inaccurate, far less regularly inaccurate, with respect to self-knowledge.

Schachter's analysis is based upon the Schachter–Singer experiment (1962), discussed in Chapter 2. There it was noted that the results of this experiment are consistent with the experimental hypothesis that, under conditions of ambiguity, subjects would label their emotional states in accord with social cues provided by experimental confederates in the 'anger' and 'euphoria' conditions. The outcome of this experiment does not, however, support any sceptical conclusion about self-knowledge of emotional states.

First, the outcome of this experiment can be readily explained in the following fashion. Subjects were genuinely angry and euphoric in the two experimental conditions, and provided accurate accounts of their psychological states.[3] Second, even if subjects' accounts of their emotional states were influenced by social cues, the sceptical conclusion would only follow if subjects are influenced by social cues in non-ambiguous situations, and if accounts based upon social cues are regularly inaccurate. The Schachter-Singer experiment provides no support for either of these claims. This is because the Schachter–Singer experiment is silent on the nature of emotion itself: consequently it can tell us nothing about the accuracy of subjects' accounts of their emotional state.

It was also noted that Schachter did provide an account of emotion itself, according to which homogeneous arousal states are constituted as different emotions by different cognitive labels. However, this analysis does not suggest that subjects regularly err in their accounts of emotion. On the contrary, it *precludes the possibility of error*. If, for example, my labelling of my arousal state as 'anger' constitutes my arousal state as anger, there is no logical room for error.

Precisely the same considerations apply to Bem's analysis of attitude avowals. If Bem's experiments are interpreted as consistent with the experimental hypothesis about the social determinants of attitude avowals they provide no support for the claim that attitude avowals are regularly inaccurate, for (being a good behaviourist) Bem remains silent on the nature of attitudes themselves and the accuracy of agent avowals of them. If attitude avowals are held to be constitutive of attitudes, the possibility of error is precluded. Neither of these studies provides any support for the sceptical claim that agent accounts are unreliable and generally inaccurate.

All the other studies documented by Nisbett and Wilson and Nisbett and Ross are studies concerned with causal judgement. They cite many experiments in social psychology that appear to show that subjects regularly fail to identify causally efficacious stimuli, and regularly appeal to causally inert stimuli in the explanation of their behaviour.[4] These studies only have bearing upon the issue of self-knowledge via two assumptions. The first is that self-knowledge of emotions, beliefs, etc. involves a form of 'theoretical inference'. According to Nisbett and Wilson (1977: 233) and Nisbett and Ross (1980: 227), subjects employ socially learned *'a priori'* causal theories about emotions, beliefs, etc. when explaining their own behaviour. The second is the popular empiricist account of the meaning of theoretical propositions, documented in Chapter 4.

According to this account, the meaning of theoretical psychological descriptions is determined by the body of empirical laws relating observable environmental stimuli and behaviour in terms of which they are defined (either instrumentally or functionally). Given this account of theoretical meaning, the sceptical conclusion immediately follows. For if self-knowledge of emotion, belief, etc.

involves theoretical description, if the meaning of theoretical descriptions is specified in terms of stimulus–response sequences, and if experimental studies demonstrate that we regularly err with respect to our judgements of stimulus causality, then it follows that we regularly err with respect to self-knowledge.

The empiricist account of theoretical meaning was dismissed as hopelessly inadequate in Chapter 4. There it was argued that theoretical psychological descriptions are not defined in terms of stimulus–response sequences, but are independently defined in terms of the intensional contents of representations directed upon intentional objects. Consequently the possible regular inaccuracy of our causal judgements cannot be held to entail the regular inaccuracy and unreliability of our self-knowledge of psychological states. A defence of the reliability and general accuracy of our accounts of the contents and objects of our beliefs, emotions, and avowed motives is entirely consistent with a recognition of the unreliability and general inaccuracy of our causal explanations of actions that make reference to such psychological states.

The second assumption of the sceptical argument may thus be dismissed as false. The first assumption also appears to be false. The notion that self-knowledge generally involves a form of 'theoretical inference' is utterly implausible. We do sometimes make inferences to our psychological states from our behaviour. However, this is usually only on the relatively rare occasions that our own behaviour is *anomalous to us*. Thus, for example, I might infer that I am envious of my colleague's promotion when I realize that I have no other reason for my hostile behaviour towards her. Yet to suppose that this sort of example is the rule rather than the exception would be to suppose that one's behaviour is *usually* anomalous to oneself. This is hard to do. I do not normally recognize that I want to secure a new position as an inference from the observed behavioural fact that I am filling out an application form for it, nor do I normally recognize my grief as an inference from my behaviour in the cemetery.

Self-knowledge as perception

However, these arguments do not yet get to the heart of the matter. For they suggest that self-knowledge involves a rather more direct form of 'internal perception'. This plays directly into the hands of the sceptic, who can argue that all forms of perception are 'theory-informed', and that our 'internal perceptions' are informed by inadequate 'folk-psychological' theories.

'Eliminative materialists' such as Paul Churchland (1979, 1984) argue that such inadequate 'folk-psychological' theories ought to be replaced by superior neurophysiological theories, and that our self-knowledge would be much improved if it came to be informed by them. Thus just as we can be taught to observe the heavens in ways informed by the Copernican rather than the Ptolemaic theory, so too we can be taught to observe our internal states in ways informed by superior neurophysiological theories.

Now this account is based upon two false assumptions. In the first place, it is simply not true that epistemically significant observations in science are theoretically informed by *explanatory theories* that are the object of observational evaluation. The Watson–Crick account of the double-helical structure of DNA was experimentally established by the X-ray photographs produced by Rosalind Franklin. Observations of these photographs were informed by the theory of X-ray diffraction, not by the Watson–Crick theory of the structure of DNA. Thus there is no reason to suppose that self-knowledge of psychological phenomena is theoretically informed by explanatory 'folk-psychological' theories.

In the second place, even if self-knowledge of intentional psychological states were informed by 'folk-psychological' theories, the possible wholescale inadequacy of our 'folk-psychological' causal explanatory accounts would not oblige us to reject our 'folk-psychological' theoretical interpretation, if, as noted in the previous section and Chapter 4, the semantics and truth conditions of theoretical descriptions are independent of the causal-explanatory propositions in which they figure. As noted in Chapter 4, very young children may be able to employ theoretical psychological descriptions of their psychological states (such as their thoughts and beliefs) before they come to grasp their causal-explanatory employment (Leslie 1988). If this is the case, their accuracy cannot be a function of the accuracy of any causal-explanatory account.

There is, however, a much more fundamental problem. Central to this conception of self-knowledge as theory-informed perception is the notion that self-knowledge is a form of perceptual discrimination of internal states that improves with increased experience and superior theory (like the ordinary perceptual skills of the astronomer and symphony conductor). According to Churchland (1984: 73): 'what is simply a dislike for someone, for a child, may divide into a mixture of jealousy, fear, and moral disapproval of someone, in the case of an honest and self-perceptive adult'.

Now there is a reasonably plausible story to be told about self-knowledge as internal perception in the case of sensations. This is because sensations such as pains and tickles occur and recur in us independently of any form of meaningful representation (of anything, including pain). Accordingly self-knowledge of sensations such as pain may be characterized as the perceptual discrimination of internal states informed by our (socially learned) theoretical concept *of* pain.

However, this sort of story is not even remotely plausible in the case of self-knowledge of intentional psychological phenomena. For emotions and beliefs etc. do not occur and recur in us independently of any form of representation. Rather they are constituted as particular emotions and beliefs etc. precisely by the forms of meaningful representation they involve. Take shame for example. It does not occur in us spontaneously and independently of representation, and then become revealed to us by our correct internal discrimination according to some socially learned theoretical label. Rather we have to learn to *be ashamed*, which means that we have to learn to represent certain classes of action (or failure to act) as personally degrading and humiliating. Once we have learned to be ashamed, we know our shame when we know that we represent our action in just this socially meaningful way. That is essentially what we know, and all that we need to know, when we know that we are ashamed.

Contra Churchland, the reason very young children cannot discriminate jealously, adult fear, and moral disapproval is not because of their lack of introspective skills, nor is it because they lack sophisticated 'folk-psychological' theories *of* such phenomena that purportedly inform adult judgements. The reason is simply because very young children are not jealous, are not afraid in adult ways, and do not express moral disapproval. They have to learn to be jealous, have adult fears, and express moral disapproval. This does not mean that they have to learn the 'folk-psychological' concepts *of* jealousy, adult fear, and moral disapproval, in order that they can make finer discriminations of their already rich and complicated psychological lives. Rather they have to learn to lead richer and more complicated psychological lives by learning to represent (and discriminate) social reality according to the conventional social ways that are constitutive of these forms of emotion in any form of social life. When they come to represent *social reality* in these ways, knowing that they do so on particular occasions is all that is involved in self-knowledge of these emotions.

Looking in the wrong direction

These points suggest that the 'eliminative materialist' strategy for the advancement of self-knowledge is radically misconceived. Let us suppose for a moment that we could discriminate psychological states by some form of internal perception informed by current neurophysiological theory. What would this tell us in the case of shame, for example? Our perceptual judgements based upon such hypothetical internal discriminations would be articulations of the intensional content and intentional direction of our neurophysiological theories about our internal states. Yet what we need to know is the intensional content and intentional object of our *shame*: the intensional content and intentional object of our representation of *social reality*. That is, any form of internal perception informed by any form of theory would be necessarily focused in the wrong direction.

It ought to be stressed that this sort of objection applies equally to contemporary defences of the accuracy of introspection or self-perception in terms of 'cognitive monitoring' (Ericsson and Simon 1984; Pope and Singer 1978; Von Cranach 1982). In order for my reflection upon internal states to generate knowledge, I must be able to successfully articulate what I have perceived, monitored (or inferred etc.). Yet this presupposes precisely the ability that such accounts are designed to explain or deny (or it presupposes an infinite regress of perceptions of perceptions etc.). What this demonstrates is that self-knowledge of emotion, belief, etc. is not analogous to any form of perception or inference. It is rather to be identified with our knowledge of the intensional contents and intentional objects of the theories that do inform our perception and inferences.

SELF-KNOWLEDGE: DESCRIPTION AND ARTICULATION

The 'theatre' of the mind

There seems to be a fundamental misconception underlying all such accounts, derived from the classical empiricist conception of psychological states. According to this conception, to be in a psychological state is to have some sort of mental object (idea, image, sense-impression, etc.) before the mind. A good many philosophers and psychologists have abandoned this 'inner-theatre' conception of psychological states (at least I hope they have). However, most appear to have retained its natural corollary: that self-knowledge of psychological states is a form of knowledge of the properties of such internal objects.

There do not appear to be any such internal objects to be known in the case of self-knowledge of psychological states.[5] What I know in the case of self-knowledge of psychological states is not the actual properties of any internal objects, nor the actual properties of the intentional objects to which my emotions, beliefs, etc. are directed, but the intensional content and intentional direction of my emotions, beliefs etc. When I know that I love my wife and that I believe that my boss's character is beyond reproach, I do not have knowledge of the properties of any inner objects, or knowledge of the actual properties of my wife and boss. I know *what* I feel and believe about *them*. If I have doubts about whether I truly love my wife or what I believe about my boss's character, I do not direct my attention to any internal states. I direct my attention to my wife and my boss.

Self-knowledge and accounting

Self-knowledge does not involve any form of inference or perception or labelling. It is nothing more or less than the ability to articulate the contents and objects of our emotions, motives, beliefs, etc. Although agents can themselves employ descriptions of their psychological states ('I was depressed' or 'I was motivated by revenge'), their accounts of their psychological states that can serve as an exploratory resource in social psychological science (and everyday life) *are not themselves descriptions of them*. Consider the following fictional but unremarkable example of psychological accounting:

> I ought not to have cheated in the exam.... I regret it more than anything else in my life. It offended the hell out of me to see those rich kids get higher grades than me. They have all the advantages ... they don't have to work as well, and they got

> all them fancy tutors. Still I shouldn't have cheated ... it makes me less of a person than them ...

In this account the speaker *expresses* her shame and anger by *articulating* their contents and objects. She does not describe her shame and anger. Agent accounts enable us to identify their psychological states by providing accounts of their contents and objects: they enable us to empirically evaluate the accuracy of theoretical descriptions of psychological states.

It was noted in Chapter 4 that our theoretical ascriptions of psychological states are linguistically modelled: theoretical descriptions of emotions, beliefs, etc. involve the ascription of intensional contents and intentional objects of representations modelled upon the sense and reference of propositions. This strongly suggests that the best theoretical model for self-knowledge of psychological states is our knowledge of the sense and reference of our utterances. This in turn suggests the implausibility of supposing that our articulation of the intensional content and intentional direction of our emotions, beliefs, etc. might be regularly inaccurate or unreliable (or universally false). For this would be like supposing that we regularly err – and that we *all* regularly err – with respect to our knowledge of the sense and intended reference of our linguistic utterances. This is hard to believe, and would be impossible to communicate if it were true.

If this is correct, then it generalizes to our self-knowledge of our actions: our knowledge of *what* we are doing. Self-knowledge of our actions is also knowledge of intensional content and intentional direction of representations. Thus in order to know that my action is aggressive or dishonest, I need to know that I represent my behaviour as directed towards the injury of another, or as involving the removal or receipt of goods or services that rightly belong to another. If self-knowledge of emotions and beliefs can be supposed to be generally accurate and reliable, then so also can our self-knowledge of our actions. Furthermore we have independent grounds (i.e. independent of the linguistic analogy) for supposing their general accuracy and reliability. It is difficult to conceive of self-knowledge of actions as regularly inaccurate and unreliable, for, as Giddens (1979: 19) notes, self-knowledge of actions is the 'very ontological condition of human life in society'.

These reflections suggest that the 'inner focus' metaphor that has dominated classical and contemporary accounts of self-knowledge ought to be abandoned. I do not know my shame, motive of revenge, or belief that the economy will go into recession by reflecting inwards ('in vacant or in pensive mood'), as many poets, philosophers, and psychologists have been wont to imagine. Self-knowledge of emotions, motives, and beliefs is externally and socially directed rather than internally and psychologically directed.

If these reflections are even approximations to the truth, two significant and perhaps surprising consequences follow. First, there is no such thing as consciousness or awareness of psychological states. We can of course be conscious or aware of our pains, sense-data, and physiological arousal, and can be conscious and aware of trees and tarantulas, persons and their problems, our actions and social relations. We are never, however, conscious or aware of our psychological states. This is because in the case of self-knowledge of physiological states, there are no objects whose properties we could be conscious of. To suppose otherwise is the illusion of many epochs. We can of course articulate the content and direction of our psychological states, and may care to call this 'consciousness of psychological states'. But that is a quite different matter.

Second, we need to abandon the common assumption that self-knowledge of psychological states will improve as a function of increased theoretical knowledge. We normally do assume with some justification that our knowledge generally increases with an increase in the complexity and sophistication of theories. If self-knowledge involved a form of theoretical inference or theoretically-informed perception, then our self-knowledge of our psychological states would increase as a function of the adequacy of our theories about our psychological states. However, self-knowledge involves neither theoretical inference nor theory-informed perception. Consequently this assumption must be resisted in the case of self-knowledge.

We may put the point in the following fashion. When I know my shame, I know that I represent my action as degrading and humiliating. This is all I know, and all I need to know, when I know my shame. I do not need to know that it is conventionally described as 'shame', and learn nothing more about my shame when I learn that it is so described. It was suggested in Chapter 2 that there would be no loss to the richness and complexity of our psychological lives if our language did not employ descriptions of our psychological states. Analogously it may be suggested that there would be no diminution or dilution of self-knowledge of our psychological lives if we did not employ descriptions of, or theories about, our psychological states. There is no logical contradiction or empirical absurdity about a form of social life in which agents lead rich psychological lives and possess a high degree of self-knowledge, but abjure descriptions of, and theories about, their psychological states.

It was also noted in Chapter 2 that agents in many primitive forms of social life do eschew descriptive discourse about psychological states, and show no theoretical interest in their 'inner lives'. We may be inclined to dismiss these forms of life precisely because they are primitive, but it may be we not they who are missing something. For it does not seem to follow that agents in these forms of life lack psychological states or self-knowledge of them, and there is no good evidence to suggest this.

Nor does it seem to follow that our self-knowledge is superior to theirs. Indeed a stronger conclusion may be suggested: it may be our self-knowledge that is inadequate. Our generation is especially well known for its introspective concerns and theories about the 'inner life' (Logan 1987). The analysis of self-knowledge advanced in this chapter suggests that any form of 'inner focus' is misdirected and distorting, and it may be the case that our contemporary introverted concerns are our greatest impediment to self-knowledge. Perhaps we are better advised to follow the Tahitians, for example, and instead focus upon our actions and social relations (Levy 1984). There may be some real folk wisdom in the aphorism that South Sea islands are good for the soul.

KNOWLEDGE OF THE SELF

Social constructionists claim that there is no such entity as 'the self' that is the object of self-knowledge, or which can be the object of scientific knowledge. They claim that 'the self' is constituted by our social discourse putatively about 'the self', or (what amounts to the same thing) that there is nothing more to 'the self' than our forms of social discourse (Kitzinger 1989).

Social constructionists are correct to claim that there is no mysterious 'inner object' that is the object of social discourse or self-knowledge. The selves that we are are just the socially constituted persons that we are: the social agents that we are, with our powers, liabilities, and potentials, and commitment to socially located identity projects. We may properly be said to have epistemically objective knowledge of our powers, liabilities, and potential, of the content of our identity projects, and of our success or failure in pursuing them. Our 'self-concept' may properly be said to be linguistically objective: it may be more or less accurate, and subject to the normal biases and distortions of any form of social knowledge. We may have an unrealistic and inaccurate estimate of our powers, liabilities, and potential; we may deceive ourselves about our commitment to (or level of commitment to) the moral careers that comprise our identity projects; and we may delude ourselves about our success or failure in pursuing them.

Many social constructionists follow Harré (1987: 49) in characterizing 'the self' as a 'theory' (as opposed to an 'entity'): 'The "self" ... is the central concept of a theory, which the persons who hold it use to impose order upon their thoughts, feelings, and actions'. This claim is ambiguous, for it may be given either an instrumentalist or realist interpretation. Our theories about the selves or persons that we are are not linguistic devices that 'impose order' by the mere 'conceptual integration' of the empirical phenomena putatively explained by them (the instrumentalist interpretation). Our theories about the selves that we are are linguistically objective descriptions of our powers, liabilities, and potential, our commitment to identity projects, and our success or failure in pursuing them (the realist interpretation).

As noted in Chapter 2, there is an important respect in which our theories about the selves that we are may be said to 'impose order' upon our 'thoughts, feeling, and actions'. Our commitments to the conventions of social collectives within which our identity projects are located provides the social evaluative matrix within which our emotions, motives, and actions are constituted. This does not, however, require that we employ a theory about these matters: it is sufficient that we have the commitments that are constitutive of this social evaluative matrix. That is, the 'theories' that do play a constitutive role with respect to our identities are not reflexively directed upon ourselves. They are directed upon our actions and social relations.

None of this is of course to deny the causal potency of our social discourse about 'the self', or to deny that such discourse may be employed (intentionally or unintentionally) by individuals or social groups to promote a variety of social, economic, or political goals (Kitzinger 1989). It is simply to deny that such forms of discourse are in any way constitutive of our selves or our psychological lives, and to maintain the (linguistic and epistemic) objectivity of our knowledge of our selves and our psychological lives.

CONCLUSION: THE SOCIAL AND THE RELATIONAL

In this short work I have tried to provide an introduction to the philosophy of social psychological science by advancing and defending a realist account of social psychological science. According to this account, our lay and scientific descriptions and explanations of human actions and psychological states may be characterized as linguistically and epistemically objective. According to this account, social psychological science aims to advance causal explanations of human actions that can be rationally evaluated by means of experiments and other forms of empirical enquiry. This account has been defended against the critical arguments of empiricists, relativists, and social constructionists.

I have also tried to stress the importance of the social dimensions of mind and action: the respects in which persons and their actions and psychological lives may be said to be socially constituted. I have tried to do this while at the same time rejecting social constructionist and relativist denials of linguistic and epistemic objectivity. It has been argued against the empiricist that actions and psychological states are not constituted by their physical dimensions, and against the social constructionist that actions and psychological states are not constituted by our linguistic descriptions of them (or our representations of them informed by linguistic descriptions). Rather it has been claimed that actions and psychological states are constituted as actions and psychological states by their social relational and representational dimensions.

The recognition of the social dimensions of mind and action does not oblige us to abandon linguistic or epistemic objectivity. It does, however, oblige us to recognize some methodological consequences. These should be neither underestimated nor exaggerated. It requires that researchers become much more sensitive to the social relational and representational dimensions of human action. It may require in many cases that researchers abandon traditional forms of laboratory experimentation (including those involving deception) in favour of field experiments or simulations. It requires that researchers become much more sensitive to the social relations and representations that are constitutive of our psychologies and personal identities, by locating these phenomena within identity projects within social collectives. It does not require that we abandon the empirical evaluation of theoretical descriptions and causal explanations in favour of some other forms of enquiry, such as linguistic or political analysis.

One important point that has been continually stressed and deserves to be repeated in conclusion is the logical independence of descriptive and explanatory issues. To affirm that human actions and psychological states have social and psychological dimensions does not entail that such phenomena have social or psychological explanations. In particular, to affirm that an action has psychological dimensions does not entail or imply that it has a psychological explanation. To affirm that an action has social dimensions does not entail or imply that it has a social explanation. Aggressive actions have psychological dimensions, but the best explanation of some instances of aggression may be in terms of non-contentful neurophysiological states (excitations of the lateral hypothalamus). Acts of suicide have social dimensions (insofar as the contents of the forms of representation constitutive of suicide are appropriated from social discourse), but the best explanation of many suicides may be in terms of psychological states such as depression. So too with psychological phenomena. The recognition of the social relational and representational dimensions of these phenomena carries no explanatory implications.

These points do, however, raise the important and interesting question: what does it mean to characterize a description or explanation as 'social', as opposed to 'psychological' or 'biological' etc.? Or, more generally, what exactly is *social* about social phenomena?

This question has been the subject of heated controversy and debate since the days of Durkheim (1895) and Weber (1922), the founding fathers of the academic discipline of sociology. Both Weber and Durkheim were concerned to delineate the 'central subject matter' of sociology, to identify those 'social facts' that enable us to clearly demarcate sociology as a unique discipline distinct from other academic disciplines such as psychology and biology: 'We must accurately distinguish social facts and show what it is that gives them their identity, if we are to avoid reducing sociology to nothing but a conventional label applied to an incoherent collection of separate disciplines' (Durkheim 1900: 27–8).

The term 'subject-matter' of sociology is ambiguous. It may refer to social phenomena that are the object of explanation in sociological science, or it may refer to the social explanations advanced within sociological science. Weber characterized the objects of explanation in sociology as 'social actions': an action is 'social' if 'by virtue of the subjective meaning attached to it by the acting individual(s) it takes into account the behaviour of others and is therefore oriented in its course' (1922: 88). However, such a characterization appears to be too restrictive. Consider a paradigm example of sociological explanation, such as Durkheim's (1897) explanation of suicide, or, strictly speaking, suicide rates, in terms of membership of social groups defined according to age, class, sex, religion, etc., and levels of 'social integration' within such groups. Weber's characterization of 'social action' would exclude many actions that may properly be characterized as suicides,[1] according to a common definition in terms of the intention to bring about one's own death (or according to Durkheim's own idiosyncratic definition in terms of 'dying as a result of an act one knows will produce one's death'). No doubt some suicidal agents do take into account the 'behaviour of others': their suicides may be conceived by them as a response to rejection by a lover, or designed to gain sympathy from others. However, it seems plain that some do not: some suicides may be motivated solely by a desire to avoid insufferable pain. That is, those phenomena that can be given a social explanation, such as suicide or suicide rates, may not be social according to any definition of the 'subject-matter' of sociology.

In consequence we might be tempted to characterize 'social phenomena' as those phenomena that can be given a social explanation. The problem with this is that there is no way of identifying social phenomena in advance of successful sociological science. We cannot say, for example, that actions such as suicide or practices such as religion are intrinsically social: we just have to wait and see if they turn out to be contingently so. That is, the best explanation of suicide or suicide rates may turn out to be psychological rather than social: these may be best explained in terms of depression or rates of depression in different social groups. Furthermore, this merely relocates the problem, for no account has been given of the difference between social and psychological explanations. Critics of sociological science might complain that explanations of suicide rates in terms of membership of social groups defined according to age, class, sex, religion, etc. reduce to psychological explanations in terms of psychological facts about typical persons of a certain age, class, sex, religion, etc. Indeed Durkheim's own expanded social explanations come very close to this: thus Durkheim (1895: 131) explains lower rates of suicide for members of certain religious groups not in terms of social integration within the group, but in terms of beliefs about the eternal punishment of suicides in hell.

One might in consequence be tempted to characterize sociology, and other disciplines such as psychology and biology, in terms of the *forms of explanation* they advance, without pretending that one had advance knowledge of the types of phenomena that are best explained in terms of them. One problem with this account, and indeed with *any* attempt to demarcate sociology as distinct from psychology and biology, is that it promotes the institutional presumption that such disciplinary boundaries are *ontologically grounded*. Thus psychologists regularly ignore social factors in advancing explanations of emotion and human intelligence, as if the fact that these phenomena are studied by psychologists somehow precludes their social explanation. Conversely, many sociologists seem to presume that social explanations can be advanced to include everything from aggression and intelligence to gender, race, and AIDS, just because these phenomena have social significance. This breeds nothing but dissension and confusion. Furthermore it still leaves open the question of the difference between social and psychological explanations: if these are formally defined in terms of the types of objects they reference, we return full circle to the definition of the 'social' as opposed to the 'psychological' and the 'biological'.

I do not have a neat answer to this question. In fact I seriously doubt if there is one. As noted in the course of this work, there are a variety of respects in which actions and psychological states may be said to be social in nature. Actions may be said to be social insofar as some actions are constituted by social relations (the decisions of jurors), some by the socially meaningful contents of participant agent representations (aggression and dishonesty), and some by the conventions of social collectives (insults). Some psychological states (e.g. beliefs) may be said to be social insofar as they are constituted as psychological states by their socially meaningful contents frequently directed upon social objects, and others (e.g. emotions and motives) also insofar as they are located within and governed by the social conventions of identity projects within social collectives. There are no doubt other respects in which such phenomena (and others) may be said to be social in nature. It is far from obvious that any of these respects in which phenomena may be described as social are conceptually primitive, and it is also doubtful if there is virtue in supposing that this is the case.

This is not to deny that all these phenomena have something in common. It may be suggested that any phenomenon may be characterized as 'social' if its description makes explicit or implicit reference to other persons (in the case of actions and psychological states attributed to individual persons) or a multiplicity of persons (in the case of social groups and collectives). This simple definition covers all the respects in which human agents and their actions and psychologies have been described as 'social' in this work.

This of course provides an answer to the question: what is *social* about social phenomena. It does not, however, provide one that allows us to clearly demarcate the domains of sociological, psychological, and biological science. For it is very difficult, for example, to provide a characterization of psychological phenomena that is logically independent of any reference to the social. Indeed one consequence of the above analysis of the 'social' is that a great many phenomena conventionally described as 'psychological', and perhaps some conventionally described as 'biological', may be described as 'social' and may have 'social' explanations. As may be obvious from the general tenor of this work, I consider this to be an important truth that tends to be obscured by artificial divisions of labour between sociologists, psychologists, and biologists (witness the frequent intellectual antagonism of biologists and psychologists to social analyses of gender and intelligence). If this causes concerns about intellectual imperialism, it perhaps ought to be pointed out that another consequence of the analysis is that many 'social' phenomena may also be described as psychological and biological, and may turn out to have psychological or biological explanations. I also consider this to be an important truth that tends to be obscured by artificial disciplinary divisions of labour (witness the intellectual outrage against the very idea of sociobiology among sociologists).

If these remarks suggest the neglect of the social by disciplines such as psychology and biology, the following are designed to suggest the neglect of the *relational* by disciplines such as sociology and social psychology.

When Durkheim (1895) tried to delineate those 'social phenomena' or 'social facts' that constitute the proper 'subject matter' of sociology, he naturally tended to focus on collective phenomena such as marriages, religious organizations, legal, commercial, and banking institutions, all of which involve social conventions and relationships. Unfortunately the most detailed illustrative example he gave, namely a crowd emotion, cannot be assimilated with the other examples, and it is in fact doubtful if it can be identified as a genuinely collective phenomenon. This is because descriptions such as 'the crowd was angry' easily reduce to descriptions of the psychological states of many (or most) of its members. Explanations of the generation or spread of emotion in a crowd need make no reference to social conventions or social relations. It may be readily explained by the fact that many or most of the members were angered by the same state of affairs (the president's speech or the linesman's decision), or by the anger of some being transmitted to the others via behavioural cues and signals.

That is, there appears to be an important difference between what may be termed an *aggregate group* and a genuine *social collective*. This is revealed for example by the different criteria we normally employ for the transtemporal identity of aggregate groups and collectives. We treat a group of individuals in the city square or at the football game last week as a different crowd from the group of individuals in the city square or at the football game this week if their membership is different. In contrast, collective institutions such as City College and the Roman Catholic Church retain their identity over time despite complete changes in their membership, so long as they maintain their conventional functions and system of social relations. If the same people return to the square or football game the following week, the same crowd has returned. The same people who got married in church may return together to the church where they were once married: they only remain married if they have maintained the system of social and legal relations constitutive of marriage.

The point of these distinctions is that even those branches of human science that have been concerned to emphasize the social have continued to neglect the relational. If the study of individual actions and psychological states has been intellectually dominated by the principle of atomism, the study of social collectives has been dominated by the logically analogous *principle of individualism*: that social collectives (however complex they may appear) are essentially nothing more than aggregates of individuals, that their identity and nature is determined by their composition.[2] Much academic sociology and social psychology continues to be dominated by the atomistic and individualist shades of Newton and Hobbes (1651), and many explanations of the dynamics of social collectives do not differ substantially in form from natural-scientific explanations of the internal dynamics of aggregate physical phenomena such as gases (think of the usual explanations of crowd emotions). It continues to neglect the relational conception of social collectivity to be found in the *New Science* of Vico (1725), the *Idea* of Herder (1784), the *Anthropologie* of Kant (1798), and the *Volkerpsychologie* of Wundt (1920).

This neglect of the relational leads to the neglect of important and exciting theoretical possibilities. In conclusion I will mention one. Margaret Gilbert (1989) has recently argued that shared properties or beliefs is not a necessary or sufficient condition of social collectivity. She argues that many social groups are constituted as collectives by their social relations, involving a 'joint commitment' to the representation of themselves as constituting a 'plural subject' of action. Thus certain actions, such as the decisions of a committee, or the judgements of a jury, may be best conceived as 'joint actions' of a 'plural subject', as opposed to an aggregation of individual actions by individual subjects. These might not appear to be interestingly different, until one considers the following theoretical possibility: that sometimes agents act for the sake of beliefs that *are quite literally not their own*. After the social negotiation of the evidence, a jury member may endorse the collective judgement of guilt by the 'plural subject' – the jury – of which she is a constitutive member, even though she individually believes in the innocence of the defendant.

Consider the conventional explanation and conventional form of experimental investigation of the 'risky shift'. Many experimental studies have suggested that individuals are more inclined to make riskier judgements in a 'group situation' than they are by themselves (Stone 1961; Kogan and Wallach 1967). The results of later experiments have been ambiguous: some have failed to replicate the effect, and others have produced the opposite effect (Cartwright 1973). The results of such experiments are usually explained in terms of the transformation of individual beliefs consequent to social interaction and negotiation (cf. the internal dynamics of a gas), and such experiments usually involve the measurement of individual attitudes and judgements prior to and after a group discussion.

Thus, for example, experimental subjects are presented with a hypothetical situation in which someone has to choose between a safe but relatively unattractive alternative and a more attractive riskier one (e.g., between a secure but dull job and an insecure but exciting one), and asked to identify the lowest odds for the success of the riskier alternative that would be accepted as sufficient to recommend it. Subjects then meet in groups to discuss the hypothetical situation and are asked to form a unanimous decision about the lowest odds for recommendation of the riskier alternative, and are later asked again individually for their identification of these odds. It was frequently found that groups made riskier decisions than individuals alone (they accepted lower odds), and that individuals tended to make riskier decisions after group interaction than before, and this was explained as an outcome of group interaction.

However, Gilbert's analysis suggests that this conception may be radically misconceived. It may be the case that at least some individuals do not change their beliefs as a result of social interaction, but come to endorse the beliefs of the 'plural subject' of which they become a member, but which they do not individually share. The fact that individuals often avow a change in belief consequent to the group discussion establishes nothing, for they may be endorsing the beliefs of the 'plural subject' of which they consider themselves to (still) be members, but which they may not as individuals share.

They may act upon such beliefs in situations where they consider themselves to be members of that 'plural subject', even if they do not individually share such beliefs. They may not do so in situations where they consider their membership of a particular 'plural subject' to be irrelevant, and may act upon their own beliefs instead. As a member of the financial steering committee of a public institution, an individual may endorse and act upon the beliefs of the 'plural subject' of which she is a member, even though she does not individually accept them. She may direct the institutional monies over which she has professional control into the stock market, if the 'plural subject' decides that this is the best way to invest monies in the current financial climate, even though the 'plural subject' does not direct her to do so and leaves her completely free to make independent investment decisions. In this way she may act upon beliefs that she literally does not share. She may also withdraw her own money from the stock market precisely because she does not individually share this belief. Of course this may create a conflict that demands resolution. However, these conflicts may very well arise and may remain unresolved.

The relational nature of social collectives such as 'plural subjects' may also explain the inconclusive results of 'replications' of 'risky-shift' experiments. Not all forms of group discussion may promote the formation of the social relations and representations that are constitutive of 'plural subjects'. Even when they do, it may be the case that individuals questioned at a later date no longer conceive of themselves as members of a 'plural subject', and reaffirm their original beliefs that they have continued to maintain as individuals.

Of course this is only a theoretical suggestion, albeit an intriguing one. The point is that such forms of explanation are largely ignored by the individualist orientation of much 'social' research, and their evaluation largely precluded by the individualist orientation of the experimental analysis of many 'social' phenomena.

Largely for the reasons documented in this conclusion, I have talked throughout this work of the potential and limits of social psychological science rather than of individual disciplines such as social psychology, general psychology, sociology, and anthropology. Indeed I doubt if there is point or profit in trying to make philosophical points about these disciplines individually. All the points that have been made apply to any discipline concerned to advance empirically-evaluated explanations of phenomena that have social relational and representational dimensions, or offer explanations of phenomena in terms of these dimensions.

My own view is that we ought to abandon traditional disciplinary distinctions, and reconstitute anew a comprehensive human science or science of persons. This would be a science of human agents that recognized the biological, psychological, and social dimensions of human agents, and the biological, psychological, and social conditions of their powers, liabilities, and potential. It would be a theoretically integrated science of human agents whose actions and psychologies are biologically incarnated and socially located.

EPILOGUE

Some critics of this short work might object that I have unfairly criticized some individuals or disciplines for failing to appreciate the virtues of a realist account of social psychological science, or for neglect of the social relational and representational dimensions of human actions and psychological states. If this is in fact the case, I am glad to hear it and happy to acknowledge my error, recognizing that such individuals or disciplines need no convincing. If it is complained that I have unfairly characterized most individuals and disciplines on these grounds, I would treat this with very considerable scepticism. I have derived the opposite impression from the literature, and from my conversations with many psychologists, sociologists, and social psychologists.

Nevertheless I am also faintly optimistic about the prospects of a change in attitude. Many professional researchers and students appear dissatisfied with the intellectual sterility of empiricism, yet continue to resist the transient temptations of relativism and social constructionism. I hope that they will find realism and social constitutionism more attractive.

If the arguments of this little volume become dated because they come in time to be directed against straw men, I would welcome such an outcome. If the arguments of this little volume become dated in any small part because they convince some researchers and students to change or at least reappraise their ingrained philosophical positions, then it will have succeeded in its purpose.

NOTES

1 SOCIAL DIMENSIONS OF ACTION

1 This way of expressing the point is liable to mislead, since philosophers employ the term 'intrinsic' (or 'internal') to reference those properties or relations that are constitutive of identity, and the term 'extrinsic' (or 'external') to reference those properties or relations that are not. The basic point may be alternatively expressed by noting that relational phenomena such as trials by jury are constituted as trials by jury by their *intrinsic* relations to phenomena *extrinsic* to them.

2 This is not of course to deny that non-linguistic animals can have goals or intentions. Their behaviours – bringing their food bowl or leash – can be purposively directed. It is to deny that they can be ascribed psychological states whose socially meaningful contents are appropriated from language. See also Chapter 2, note 2.

3 Examples of 'violent stimuli' are guns, pictures of Rocky or Rambo, etc.: i.e. stimuli associated with or representative of violence.

4 There are those (e.g. Gergen 1989) who claim that our 'theoretical' discourse about our actions and psychological states is non-descriptive. This claim is considered and rejected in Chapter 2, pp. 44–5.

5 The presence of a descriptive term in the language of another culture that translates as 'aggression' or 'dishonesty' in our own is of course good evidence that there is aggression and dishonesty in that culture. It is not, however, sufficient evidence. There may, for example, also be descriptions that translate as 'prayer' and 'marriage', even though they have all become atheists and abandoned the practice of marriage.

6 This question is discussed further in Chapter 2, pp. 54–5, where an alternative perspective is presented.

2 SOCIAL DIMENSIONS OF MIND

1 I do not pretend that these are adequate or comprehensive accounts of the socially meaningful contents of shame and revenge, nor do I pretend that this is true of my accounts of the contents of other emotions and motives in this chapter. The characterizations employed are in-

tended as economical approximations that are sufficient for the purposes of the present analysis. For a much richer account of these matters, see Sabini and Silver (1982).

2 This of course implies that we cannot attribute many emotions and motives, or beliefs, to non-linguistic animals. It might be objected that we can attribute beliefs or emotions to at least some non-linguistic animals. In one respect this is true. All animals may be said to be able to employ concepts or have beliefs to the degree that they can re-identify and discriminate phenomena via sense-perception, and anticipate outcomes on the basis of associated past experience. Thus the president's dog may be said to have 'beliefs' to the degree that it can recognize the president coming up the path and anticipate being taken for a walk on his return. It cannot, however, be said to believe *that it is the president*, or hope *that it will be taken for a walk*. For such linguistically informed beliefs can only be attributed to beings that can grasp the meaning of the descriptions 'president' and 'walk'. The dog may be said to have a 'concept' of the president to the degree that it can recognize him coming up the path, but not in the sense that it grasps the truth conditions of the description 'president'. A zebra may be said to be afraid in the sense that it can sense signs of danger and be aroused by them, but a zebra cannot be said to be ashamed of being caught with its family in a vulnerable position.

If someone still wants to insist that contentful beliefs can be attributed to non-linguistic animals, I don't mind. Many of the points of this chapter can then be extended to cover the animal kingdom also. Those points that depend upon the grasp of linguistic distinctions would then only apply to those linguistically informed beliefs of human agents (and perhaps some chimpanzees such as Washoe) that Dennett (1978) calls 'opinions'.

3 This is not to deny that emotions can be directed upon other emotions: I can be ashamed of my fear and indeed ashamed of my shame. Nor is it to deny that emotions can be directed upon phenomena other than actions and social relations: I may be ashamed of my obesity and fearful of my heart flutterings. It is to deny that any emotion is constituted as that particular emotion by the representation *of that particular emotion itself*.

4 This is not to endorse Schachter's claim that different emotions are physiologically homogeneous. I doubt in fact if this is the case. It is to claim that our emotions are not themselves constituted as different emotions by physiological differences. If they are in fact physiologically heterogeneous or homogeneous, this is an additional interesting fact about them.

5 This is not to deny that DSM-III includes representational criteria, which of course it does. However, according to DSM-III, there is no representational state that is a necessary condition of depression, nor indeed is it a necessary condition of depression that the agent represents reality in any way at all.

6 This is not of course to deny that such states are incarnated, only that

their mode of neurophysiological incarnation is not constitutive of their identity.

7 This is not to claim that all their actions and psychological states can be explained in these terms, far less all their properties and behaviour. Persons are also biological, chemical, and physical entities, and many of their properties and behaviours can be explained (universally or generally) in terms of their biological, chemical, and physical properties.

3 CAUSAL EXPLANATION

1 Invariant correlation under conditions of closure is not, however, necessary to establish a causal power, if, as argued in this chapter, some powers have enabling conditions only, and others are under the control of agents. To ascribe a causal power to an entity is only to say that it *can* generate an effect under certain conditions; this can be established by occasional rather than invariant manifestations of its power.

2 This argument, the only good one I know, comes from Kant (1787). For a more detailed discussion see Greenwood (1990).

3 It might be objected that this is because of the random assignment of personally different subjects to experimental conditions: some subjects may simply not be liable to be aggressive in the presence of 'violent stimuli', but the aggressive actions of others may be determined by stimulus conditions. This may of course be the case. The point is that the logic of experimental design does not presume this, nor does the outcome of such experiments establish it.

4 THEORY AND OBSERVATION

1 Although not of Watson (1924), who was not influenced by logical positivism or scientific empiricism (although no doubt he was influenced by the general empiricist tradition).

2 This is not of course to deny that the accuracy of descriptions of empirical correlations can be treated as one means of evaluating the accuracy of theoretical descriptions employed in explanations of them. It is to deny that the truth conditions of descriptions of empirical correlations and theoretical descriptions employed to explain them can be identified (cf. the *Quine–Duhem* thesis, this chapter pp. 90–1). The accuracy of descriptions of empirical correlations is not a sufficient condition of the accuracy of theoretical descriptions employed in explanations of them (although it may sometimes be treated as sufficient *evidence* for their accuracy), and the accuracy of theoretical descriptions is not a sufficient condition of the accuracy of descriptions of empirical correlations they purport to explain.

3 In this respect theoretical propositions may be said to be 'partially interpreted' and 'open' to further interpretation: the partial theoretical model is open to further interpretation.

4 Of course reference to the composition and structure of DNA and water

alone is insufficient to provide illuminating explanations of heredity and variation and the properties of water: this requires an account of how the composition and structure of these phenomena are implicated in their causal powers.

5 I don't endorse this popular claim about the semantics of pain ascriptions, and in fact doubt its adequacy. I only claim that it has a certain plausibility not shared by analogous accounts of the semantics of psychological state ascriptions.

5 EXPERIMENTATION

1 Of course not all treatments whose efficacies are the objects of experimental evaluation are professional treatments: i.e. forms of therapy employed by mental health professionals. Some are genuinely experimental treatments. However, since most of them are professional therapies, or are experimental combinatory 'packages' of such therapies, I employ this term for reasons of convenience to designate treatments employed in experimental groups whose theoretical efficacy is the object of experimental evaluation.

2 This is not to underestimate the very real problems posed by this requirement: therapists employing 'control treatments' in control groups are rarely committed to their efficacy, far less to the proposition that such 'treatments' are at least as efficacious as professional ones. For a discussion of some possible solutions, see Greenwood (1989), Chapter 13.

6 ACCOUNTING

1 I use the term 'mental states' to include both non-intentional sensational phenomena such as pains and sense data, and intentional psychological or cognitive states such as emotions, motives, and beliefs. I use the terms 'psychological' and 'cognitive' interchangeably to designate intentional phenomena. According to this employment, nonlinguistic animals may be ascribed representational states such as goals and intentions, insofar as their behaviour is purposively directed, but not (socially meaningful) contentful states such as beliefs, motives, and most emotions. See Chapter 2, note 2, and this Chapter, note 5.

2 The work of Freud is not included as grounds for scepticism because the work of Freud is in fact rarely cited as grounds for scepticism, no doubt because of popular doubts about the epistemic objectivity or viability of Freud's theories. In any case Freud never denied the *ability* of agents to have self-knowledge of their psychological lives: he only postulated various forms of impediment to it, such as sexual repression. In fact it is a presupposition – and the hope and promise – of the psychoanalytic endeavour that agents can – through therapy – come to have self-knowledge of psychological states that they previously denied.

3 See Chapter 2, pp. 41–2.

4 It is worth noting that many of these experiments have been strongly criticized on methodological grounds. For an up-to-date review of these critiques, see White (1988).

5 This claim perhaps deserves further clarification in relation to other claims made in this work, in order to avoid possible misinterpretation. To claim that there do not appear to be any internal objects to be known in the case of self-knowledge of psychological states is not of course to claim that there are no such things as psychological states such as beliefs, emotions, and motives. It is only to claim that our knowledge of these psychological states does not involve any form of perception of 'internal states'.

It is also to suggest (although this claim is logically independent of the first) that psychological states such as beliefs, emotions, and motives are not themselves 'internal states' of human agents, but complex properties of them. To ascribe such contentful states to ourselves and others is not to describe mysterious 'internal states' that have semantic properties: it is to ascribe to the agent a linguistically informed social competence. We ascribe contentful psychological states to human agents because their lives are given meaning as well as purpose and direction by the contents of their linguistic commentaries upon the natural and social psychological world.

In order for any organism to have the concept of a lion, it must be able (at least) to represent entities as lions in the sense that it can re-identify and discriminate lions (and anticipate things about them in the light of its experience etc.). In order for an organism to believe that something is a lion, it must be able to represent entities as lions in the sense that it can recognize that they satisfy the truth conditions of the description 'lion'. In order to do the former, an organism must be able to process information about the world. In order to do the latter, the organism must be able to process linguistic meaning. We regularly attribute the former competence to all animals, but only the latter to humans (and perhaps some chimpanzees such as Washoe).

It is not a logically necessary condition of either competence that an organism processes information or linguistic meaning by means of *internal states of the brain that can themselves be ascribed semantic properties.* Some, most notably Fodor (1975), have argued on theoretical and empirical grounds that this is in fact the case with respect to both the processing of information and linguistic meaning. Others, notably Churchland (1979, 1991), Stich (1983) and Stich *et al.* (1991), have argued on theoretical and empirical grounds that this is not the case with respect to either the processing of information or linguistic meaning.

It is of course these 'internal' states of our brain and their 'internal' processing that enable us to have beliefs, emotions, and motives: they enable us to represent something as being the case, as degrading and humiliating in the light of our identity projects, and as restitution for a prior injury. These forms of representation that we attribute to linguistically competent persons are themselves contentful, but they are not to be identified with any 'internal' states of the brain (with or without semantic properties).

This suggests that much of the debate about the future of 'folk-psychology' and self-knowledge confuses quite separate issues. The psychological states that we reference in explanations of human action are not to be identified with the 'sub-personal' states (Dennett 1988) processed by the brain that enable us to have beliefs, emotions, motives, etc. It may very well be the case that references to 'beliefs' (or 'opinions' (Dennett 1978)) conceived as complex properties of persons are ineliminable from our best explanations of human action, but that 'beliefs' conceived as 'internal' brain states with semantic properties are eliminable from our best explanations of cognitive processing. It may well be the case that we can provide generally-accurate and reliable accounts of our 'beliefs' (or 'opinions') when these are conceived as complex properties of persons implicated in the generation of human action, but that we have very limited knowledge of our 'beliefs' conceived as 'internal' brain states implicated in cognitive processing.

It might be objected that we must identify both forms of 'belief' if we are to link perception and action based upon cognitive processing. We can do it that way of course, but we are not obliged to. All that we are required to do is to recognize that the cognitive processing of 'internal' brain states enables us to perceive things and grasp meanings and have beliefs (or opinions), emotions, and motives.

CONCLUSION

1 This point is made by Margaret Gilbert (1989). My reading of this excellent work provided the stimulus for much of the discussion in this conclusion.

2 This is not to deny that sociologists and social psychologists discriminate different kinds of groups in terms of a variety of properties, including their structure, function, rule and role systems, etc. Of course they do. It is to claim that many conceive of all these groups as more or less complex varieties of aggregate groups: i.e. as more or less complex varieties of this basic ontological kind.

REFERENCES

Abramson, L.Y., Metalsky, G.I., and Alloy, L.B. (1989) 'Hopelessness depression: a theory-based subtype of depression', *Psychological Review* 96: 358–72.

Altschule, M.D. (1965) 'Acedia: its evolution from deadly sin to psychiatric syndrome', *British Journal of Psychiatry* 111: 117–19.

American Psychiatric Association (1980) *Diagnostic and Statistical Manual of Mental Disorders*, 3rd edn, Washington, DC: American Psychiatric Association.

Anderson, J.R. (1981) 'Concepts, propositions, and schemata: what are the cognitive units?', in J.H. Flowers (ed.) *Nebraska Symposium on Motivation: Cognitive Processes*, vol. 28, Lincoln: University of Nebraska Press.

Arendt, H. (1964) *Eichmann in Jerusalem: A Report on the Banality of Evil*, New York: Viking.

Armstrong, D.M. (1968) *A Materialist Theory of the Mind*, London: Routledge & Kegan Paul.

Asch, S.E. (1951) 'Effects of group pressure upon the modification and distortion of judgements', in H. Guetzkow (ed.) *Groups, Leadership, and Men*, Pittsburgh: Carnegie Press.

Austin, J.L. (1962) *How to Do Things with Words*, Oxford: Oxford University Press.

Barnes, B. (1977) *Interests and the Growth of Knowledge*, London: Routledge & Kegan Paul.

Baron, R.A. and Egglcston, R.J. (1972) 'Performance on the "aggression machine": motivation to help or harm?' *Psychonomic Science* 26: 321–2.

Baumrind, D. (1964) 'Some thoughts on ethics of research: after reading Milgram's "Behavioral study of obedience"', *American Psychologist* 19: 421–3.

Bell, P.B. and Staines, P.J. (1981) *Reasoning and Argument in Psychology*, London: Routledge & Kegan Paul.

Beloff, J. (1973) *Psychological Sciences*, London: Crosby Lockwood Staples.

Bem, D.J. (1967) 'Self-perception: an alternative interpretation of cognitive dissonance phenomena', *Psychological Review* 74: 183–200.

Berkeley, G. (1710) *Treatise Concerning the Principles of Human Knowledge*.

Berkowitz, L. and Donnerstein, E. (1982) 'External validity is more than skin deep: some answers to criticisms of laboratory experiments', *American Psychologist* 37: 245–57.

Berkowitz, L. and LePage, A. (1967) 'Weapons as aggression-eliciting stimuli', *Journal of Personality and Social Psychology* 7: 202–7.

Berne, E. (1970) *Games People Play*, London: Penguin.

Bernstein, D.A. and Nietzel, M.T. (1977) 'Demand characteristics in behavior modification: the natural history of a "nuisance"', in M. Hersen, R.M. Eisler, and P.M. Miller (eds) *Progress in Behavior Modification*, vol. 4, New York: Academic Press.

Bhaskar, R. (1975) *A Realist Theory of Science*, Leeds: Leeds Books.

Bloor, D. (1976) *Knowledge and Social Imagery*, London: Routledge & Kegan Paul.

Borkovec, T.D. and Nau, S.D. (1972) 'Credibility of analogue therapy rationales', *Journal of Behaviour Therapy and Experimental Psychiatry*: 3257–60.

Boucher, J. (1979) 'Culture and emotion', in J. Marsella *et al.* (eds) *Perspectives on Cross-Cultural Psychology*, London: Academic Press.

Braithwaite, R.B. (1953) *Scientific Explanation*, Cambridge: Cambridge University Press.

Breakwell, G. (ed.) (1983) *Threatened Identities*, New York: Wiley.

Bridgeman, P.W. (1927) *The Logic of Modern Physics*, New York: Macmillan.

Broadbent, D.E. (1957) 'A mechanical model for human attention and immediate memory', *Psychological Review* 64: 205–15.

Brown, H.I. (1977) *Perception, Theory, and Commitment*, Chicago: University of Chicago Press.

Brunswick, E. (1955) 'Representative design and probabilistic theory in a functional psychology', *Psychological Review* 62: 193–217.

Campbell, D.T. and Stanley, J.C. (1966) *Experimental and Quasi-Experimental Designs for Research*, Chicago: Rand McNally.

Campbell, N. (1921) *What is Science?* New York: Dover Publications.

Carnap, R. (1928) *Der Logische Aufbau der Welt*, Berlin.

—— (1966) *Philosophical Foundations of Physics* (ed. M. Gardner), New York: Basic Books.

Cartwright, D. (1973) 'Determinants of scientific progress: the case of the risky shift', *American Psychologist* 28: 222–31.

Chapanis, A. (1967) 'The relevance of laboratory studies to practical situations', *Ergonomics* 10: 557–77.

Churchland, P.M. (1979) *Realism and the Plasticity of Mind*, Cambridge: Cambridge University Press.

—— (1984) *Matter and Consciousness*, Cambridge, Mass.: MIT Press.

—— (1991) 'Folk psychology and the explanation of human behavior', in J.D. Greenwood (ed.) *The Future of Folk Psychology: Intentionality and Cognitive Science*, Cambridge: Cambridge University Press.

Clark, J.M. and Paivio, A. (1989) 'Observational and theoretical terms in psychology', *American Psychologist* 44: 500–12.

Conrad, E. and Maul, T. (1981) *Introduction to Experimental Psychology*, New York: Wiley.

Cooper, J. (1976) 'Deception and role-playing: on telling the good guys from the bad guys', *American Psychologist* 31: 605–10.

Craig, W. (1956) 'The replacement of auxiliary expressions', *Philosophical Review* 65: 35–55.

Davitz, J.R. (1969) *The Language of Emotion*, New York: Academic Press.

Dennett, D. (1978) *Brainstorms*, Cambridge, Mass.: MIT Press.

—— (1988) *The Intentional Stance*, Cambridge, Mass.: MIT Press.

De Waele, J.P. (1971) *La Methode des Cas Programmes*, Brussels: Dessart.

Duhem, P. (1906) *La Theories Physique: son Object et sa Structure*, Paris.

Durkheim, E. (1895/1968) *Les Regles de la Methode Sociologique*, Paris: Presses Universitaire de France.

—— (1897/1967) *Le Suicide: Etude de Sociologie*, Paris: Presses Universitaire de France.

—— (1900) 'La sociologia ed il suo dominio scientifico', *Revista Italiana di Sociologia* 4.

Elms, A.C. (1975) 'The crisis of confidence in social psychology', *American Psychologist* 30: 967–76.

Ericsson, K.A. and Simon, H.A. (1984) *Protocol Analysis*, Cambridge, Mass.: MIT Press.

Eysenck, H.J. (1952) 'The effects of psychotherapy: an evaluation', *Journal of Consulting Psychology* 16: 319–24.

Farrington, D.P. and Kidd, R.F. (1977) 'Is financial dishonesty a rational decision?', *British Journal of Social and Clinical Psychology* 16: 139–46.

Feigl, H. (1970) 'Beyond peaceful coexistence', in R.H. Steuwer (ed.) *Minnesota Studies in the Philosophy of Science: V*, Minneapolis: University of Minnesota Press.

Feyerabend, P.K. (1975) *Against Method*, London: New Left Books.

Findley-Jones, R. (1987) 'Accidie and melancholy in a clinical context', in R. Harré (ed.) *The Social Construction of Emotion*, Oxford: Basil Blackwell.

Flanagan, D. (1984) *The Science of the Mind*, Cambridge: MIT Press.

Fodor, J.A. (1975) *The Language of Thought*, Harvard: Harvard University Press.

—— (1984) 'Observation reconsidered', *Philosophy of Science* 51: 23–43.

Forward, J., Canter, R. and Kirsch, N. (1976) 'Role enactment and deception methodologies: alternative paradigms?', *American Psychologist* 31: 595–604.

Frank, J.D. (1974) 'Psychotherapy: the restoration of morale', *American Journal of Psychotherapy* 131: 271–4.

Freedman, J.L. (1969) 'Role-playing: psychology by consensus', *Journal of Personality and Social Psychology* 13: 107–14.

Gauld, A. and Shotter, J. (1977) *Human Action and its Psychological Investigation*, London: Routledge & Kegan Paul.

Geach, P. (1975) 'Teleological explanation', in S. Korner (ed.) *Explanation*, Oxford: Basil Blackwell.

Gergen, K.J. (1973) 'Social psychology as history', *Journal of Personality and Social Psychology* 26: 309–20.

—— (1978) 'Experimentation in social psychology: a reappraisal', *European Journal of Social Psychology*, 8: 507–27.

—— (1982) *Towards Transformation in Social Knowledge*, New York: Springer-Verlag.

—— (1985) 'The social construction movement in modern psychology', *American Psychologist* 40: 266–75.

—— (1989) 'Warranting voice and the elaboration of the self', in J. Shotter and K.J. Gergen (eds) *Texts of Identity*, Newbury Park: Sage.

Giddens, A. (1979) *Central Problems of Social Theory*, Berkeley: University of California Press.

Gilbert, M. (1989) *On Social Facts*, London: Routledge & Kegan Paul.

Ginsburg, G.P., Brenner, M., and von Cranach, M. (eds) (1985) *Discovery Strategies in the Psychology of Action*, London: Academic Press.

Goffmann, E. (1959) *The Presentation of Self in Everyday Life*, New York: Doubleday.

—— (1961) *Asylums*, New York: Doubleday.

Greenwald, A.G. (1975) 'On the inconclusiveness of "crucial" cognitive tests of dissonance versus self-perception theories', *Journal of Experimental Social Psychology* 11: 490–9.

Greenwood, J.D. (1989) *Explanation and Experiment in Social Psychological Science*, New York: Springer-Verlag.

—— (1990) 'Kant's third antinomy: agency and causal explanation', *International Philosophical Quarterly* 30: 43–57.

—— (forthcoming) *Personal Identity and the Social Dimensions of Mind*.

Hacking, I. (1983) *Representing and Intervening*, Cambridge: Cambridge University Press.

Hallpike, C. (1979) *Foundations of Primitive Thought*, Oxford: Clarendon Press.

Hanay, C., Banks, W.C., and Zimbardo, P.G. (1973) 'Interpersonal dynamics in a simulated prison', *International Journal of Criminology and Penology* 1: 69–97.

Hanson, N.R. (1958) *Patterns of Discovery*, Cambridge: Cambridge University Press.

Harré, R. (1970) *The Principles of Scientific Thinking*, Chicago: Chicago University Press.

—— (1972) *The Philosophies of Science*, Oxford: Oxford University Press.

—— (1983) *Personal Being*, Oxford: Basil Blackwell.

—— (1987) 'The social construction of selves', in K. Yardley and T. Honess (eds) *Self and Identity*, New York: Wiley.

Harré, R. and Madden, E.H. (1975) *Causal Powers*, Oxford: Basil Blackwell.

Harré, R. and Secord, P.F. (1972) *The Explanation of Social Behaviour*, Oxford: Basil Blackwell.

Harris, P.L. (1989) *Children and Emotion*, Oxford: Basil Blackwell.

Heelas, P. (1981) 'Introduction: Indigenous psychologies', in P. Heelas and A. Lock (eds) *Indigenous Psychologies*, London: Academic Press.

Hempel, C.G. (1965) *Aspects of Scientific Explanation*, New York: Free Press.

—— (1966) *Philosophy of Natural Science*, Englewood Cliffs: Prentice-Hall.

Hempel, C.G. and Oppenheim, P. (1948) 'Studies of the logic of explanation', *Philosophy of Science* 15: 135–75.

Henschel, R.L. (1980) 'The purposes of laboratory experimentation and the virtues of deliberate artificiality', *Journal of Experimental Social Psychology* 16: 466–78.

Herder, J.G. (1784) *Idea Towards a Philosophy of History*.

Herskovits, M.J. (1948) *Man and His Works*, London.

Hesse, M.B. (1976) 'Models versus paradigms in the natural sciences', in L. Collins (ed.) *The Use of Models in the Social Sciences*, London: Tavistock Press.

Hobbes, T. (1651) *Leviathan*.

Hofling, C.K., Brotzman, E., Dalrymple, S., Graves, N., and Pierce, C.M. (1966) 'An experimental study in nurse–physician relationships', *The Journal of Mental and Nervous Disease* 143: 171–80.

Holmes, D.S. and Bennett, D.H. (1974) 'Experiments to answer questions raised by the use of deception in psychological research: I. Role-playing as an alternative to deception; II. Effectiveness of debriefing after deception; III. Effect of informed consent upon deception', *Journal of Personality and Social Psychology* 29: 358–67.

Horowitz, I.A. and Rothschild, B.H. (1970) 'Conformity as a function of deception and role-playing', *Journal of Personality and Social Psychology* 14: 224–6.

Hull, C.L. (1943) *Principles of Behavior*, New York: Appleton-Century-Crofts.

Hume, D. (1739) *A Treatise on Human Nature*.

Johnson-Laird, P.N. (1983) *Mental Models*, Cambridge: Cambridge University Press.

Jourard, S.M. (1968) *Disclosing Man to Himself*, New York: Litton.

Kane, T.R., Joseph, J.P., and Tedeschi, J.T. (1976) 'Person perception and the Berkowitz paradigm for the study of aggression', *Journal of Personality and Social Psychology* 6: 663–73.

Kant, I. (1787) *Critique of Pure Reason*.

—— (1798) *Anthropologie in Pragmatischer Hinsicht*.

Kemper, T.D. (1978) *A Social Interactional Theory of Emotions*, New York: Wiley.

Kimble, G.A. (1989) 'Psychology from the standpoint of a generalist', *American Psychologist* 44: 491–9.

Kitzinger, C. (1989) 'Liberal humanism as an ideology of social control: the regulation of lesbian identities', in J. Shotter and K.J. Gergen (eds) *Texts of Identity*, Newbury Park: Sage.

Kogan, N. and Wallach, M.A. (1967) 'Risk-taking as a function of the situation, the person, and the group', in G. Mandler (ed.) *New Directions in Psychology II*, New York: Holt, Rinehart, & Winston.

Kuhn, T. (1970) *The Structure of Scientific Revolutions*, 2nd edn, Chicago: University of Chicago Press.

Lachman, R., Lachman, J. and Butterfield, E. (1979) *Cognitive Psychology and Information Processing*, New Jersey: Erlbaum.

Lakatos, I. (1970) 'Falsification and the methodology of scientific research programmes', in I. Lakatos and A. Musgrave (eds) *Criticism and the Growth of Knowledge*, Cambridge: Cambridge University Press.

Latané, B. and Darley, J.M. (1970) *The Unresponsive Bystander: Why Doesn't He Help?*, New York: Appleton-Century-Crofts.

Lazarus, R.S. (1984) 'On the primacy of cognition', *American Psychologist* 39: 124–9.

Ledwidge, B. (1978) 'Cognitive behavior modification: a step in the wrong direction?', *Psychological Bulletin* 85: 353–75.

Leslie, A.M. (1988) 'Some implications of pretence for mechanisms underlying the child's theory of mind', in J.W. Astington, P.L. Harris, and D.R. Olson (eds) *Developing Theories of Mind*, Cambridge: Cambridge University Press.

Levy, R. (1984) 'Emotion, knowing, and culture', in R. Shweder and R. LeVine (eds) *Culture Theory: Essays on Mind, Self, and Emotion*, Cambridge: Cambridge University Press.

Lewis, D. (1972) 'Psychophysical and theoretical identifications', *Australian Journal of Philosophy* 50: 249–58.

Lewis, M. and Saarni, C. (1985) 'Culture and emotion', in M. Lewis and C. Saarni (eds) *The Socialization of Emotion*, London: Plenum.

Locke, J. (1690) *An Essay Concerning Human Understanding*.

Logan, R.D. (1987) 'Historical change in prevailing sense of self', in K. Yardley and T. Honess (eds) *Self and Identity*, New York: Wiley.

Louch, A. (1967) *Explanation and Human Action*, Oxford: Basil Blackwell.

MacCorquodale, K. and Meehl, P.E. (1948) 'On a distinction between hypothetical constructs and intervening variables', *Psychological Review* 55: 95–107.

Malan, D.H. (1975) 'Psychodynamic changes in untreated neurotic patients', *Archives of General Psychiatry* 32: 110–26.

Manicas, P.T. and Secord, P.F. (1983) 'Implications for psychology of the new philosophy of science', *American Psychologist* 38: 399–413.

Margolis, J. (1984) Philosophy of Psychology, Englewood Cliffs: Prentice-Hall.

Milgram, S. (1974) *Obedience to Authority*, New York: Harper & Row.

Mill, J.S. (1863) *Utilitarianism*.

Miller, A.G. (1972) 'Role-playing: an alternative to deception? A review of the evidence', *American Psychologist* 27: 623–36.

Mixon, D. (1972) 'Instead of deception', *Journal for the Theory of Social Behaviour*, 2: 145–77.

—— (1980) 'The place of habit in the control of action', *Journal for the Theory of Social Behaviour*, 10: 169–86.

Mook, D. (1983) 'In defence of external validity', *American Psychologist* 38: 379–87.

Morsbach, H. and Tyler, W.J. (1976) 'Some Japanese–Western linguistic differences concerning dependency needs: the case of "amae"', in R. Harré (ed.) *Life Sentences*, New York: Wiley.

Myers, F. (1979) 'Emotions and the self', *Ethos* 7: 343–70.

Nagel, E. (1939) *Principles of the Theory of Probability*, Chicago: Chicago University Press.

—— (1961) *The Structure of Science*, London: Routledge & Kegan Paul.

Neurath, O. (1932) 'Protokollsatze', *Erkenntnis* 3.

Newell, A., Shaw, J.C. and Simon, H.A. (1958) 'Elements of a theory of problem-solving', *Psychological Review* 65: 151–66.

Nisbett, R.E. and Ross, L. (1980) *Human Inference: Strategies and Shortcomings of Social Judgement*, Englewood Cliffs: Prentice-Hall.

Nisbett, R.E. and Wilson, T.D. (1977) 'Telling more than we can know: verbal reports on mental processes', *Psychological Review* 84: 231–59.

Olson, D. and Astington, J. (1986) 'Children's acquisition of metalinguistic and metacognitive verbs', in W. Demopoulos and A. Marras (eds) *Language Learning and Concept Acquisition*, Norwood, N.J.: Ablex.

Olson, T. and Christiansen, G. (1966) *The Grindstone Experiment: Thirty One Hours*, Toronto: Canadian Friends Service Committee.

Orne, M.T. (1962) 'On the social psychology of the psychological experiment: with particular reference to demand characteristics and their implications', *American Psychologist* 17: 776–83.

Paivio, A. (1986) *Mental Representations: A Dual Coding Approach*, Oxford: Oxford University Press.

Perrin, S. and Spencer, C. (1980) 'The Asch effect – a child of its time?', *Bulletin of the British Psychological Society* 32: 405–6.

Pope, K.S. and Singer, J.L. (eds) (1978) *The Stream of Consciousness*, New York: Plenum Press.

Popper, K.R. (1959) *The Logic of Scientific Discovery*, London: Hutchinson.

Pylyshyn, Z.W. (1984) *Computation and Cognition*, Cambridge, Mass.: MIT Press.

Quine, W.V.O. (1953) 'Two dogmas of empiricism', in *From a Logical Point of View*, Cambridge, Mass.: Harvard University Press.

Quine, W.V.O. and Ullian, J.S. (1970) *The Web of Belief*, New York: Random House.

Rorty, R. (1979) *Philosophy and the Mirror of Nature*, Oxford: Basil Blackwell.

Rosenberg, A. (1980) *Sociobiology and the Preemption of Social Science*, Baltimore: Johns Hopkins University Press.

Rosenberg, M.J. (1969) 'The conditions and consequences of evaluation apprehension', in R. Rosenthal and R. Rosnow (eds) *Artifact in Behavioral Research*, New York: Academic Press.

Rosenthal, R. (1976) *Experimenter effects in Behavioral Research*, 2nd edn, New York: Appleton-Century-Crofts.

Sabini, J. and Silver, M. (1982) *Moralities of Everyday Life*, Oxford: Oxford University Press.

Salmon, W.C. (1971) 'Statistical explanation', in W.C. Salmon *et al.* (eds) *Statistical Explanation and Statistical Relevance*, Pittsburgh: University of Pittsburgh Press.

Sartre, J.P. (1948) *Existentialism and Humanism* (trans. P. Mairet), London.

Sayre-McCord, G. (ed.) (1989) *Essays on Moral Realism*, Ithaca: Cornell University Press.

Schachter, S. (1965) 'The interaction of cognitive and physiological determinants of emotional state', in P.H. Leidermann and D. Shapiro (eds) *Psychobiological Approaches to Social Behaviour*, London: Tavistock.

Schachter, S. and Singer, S. (1962) 'Cognitive, social, and physiological determinants of emotional state', *Psychological Review* 69: 379–99.

Schlick, M. (1936) 'Meaning and verification', *Philosophical Review* 45.

Secord, P.F. (1983) 'The behavior identity problem in generalizing from experiments', *American Psychologist* 37: 1408.

—— (1990) '"Subject" versus "Person" in social psychological research', in R. Bhaskar (ed.) *Harré and His Critics*, Oxford: Basil Blackwell.

Shapere, D. (1964) 'Meaning and scientific change', in R.G. Colodny (ed.) *Mind and Cosmos*, Pittsburgh: University of Pittsburgh Press.

Shotter, J. (1989) 'Social accountability and selfhood', in J. Shotter and K.J. Gergen (eds) *Texts of Identity*, Newbury Park: Sage.

Simon, H.A. and Kaplan, C.A. (1989) 'Foundations of cognitive science', in M.I. Posner (ed.) *Foundations of Cognitive Science*, Cambridge, Mass.: MIT Press.

Skinner, B.F. (1953) *Science and Human Behavior*, New York: Macmillan.

—— (1974) *About Behaviorism*, New York: Knopf.

Smith, J.L. (1975) 'A games analysis for attitude change: use of role enactment situations for model development', *Journal for the Theory of Social Behaviour* 5: 63–79.

Stevenson, C.L. (1944) *Ethics and Language*.

Stich, S. (1983) *From Folk Psychology to Cognitive Science: The Case Against Belief*, Cambridge, Mass.: MIT Press.

Stich, S., Ramsey, W., and Garon, J. (1991) 'Connectionism, eliminativism, and the future of folk psychology', in J.D. Greenwood (ed.) *The Future of Folk Psychology: Intentionality and Cognitive Science*, Cambridge: Cambridge University Press.

Stone, J.A.F. (1961) 'A comparison of individual and group decisions involving risk', Unpublished Master's Thesis, School of Industrial Management, MIT.

Strong, S.R. (1978) 'Social psychological approach to psychotherapy research', in S. Garfield and A. Bergin (eds) *Handbook of Psychotherapy and Behavior Change*, 2nd edn, New York: Wiley.

Taylor, C. (1977) 'What is human agency?', in T. Mischel (ed.), *The Self: Psychological and Philosophical Issues*, Oxford: Basil Blackwell.

Titchener, E.B. (1897) *An Outline of Psychology*, New York: Harcourt, Brace.

Tolman, E. (1932) *Purposive Behavior in Animals and Men*, New York: Century.

Toulmin, S. (1953) *The Philosophy of Science*, London: Hutchinson.

Triandis, H. (1980) *Handbook of Cross-Cultural Psychology*, Boston: Allyn & Bacon.

van Frassen, B.C. (1980) *The Scientific Image*, Oxford: Oxford University Press.

Vico, G.B. (1725) *Principii D'Una Scienza Nuova*.

Von Cranach, M. (1982) 'The psychological study of goal-directed action: basic issues', in M. Von Cranach and R. Harré (eds) *The Analysis of Action*, Cambridge: Cambridge University Press.

Vygotsky, L.S. (1962) *Thought and Language*, Cambridge: MIT Press.

Waismann, F. (1945) 'Verifiability', *Proceedings of the Aristotelian Society*, Supp. vol. 19: 119–50.

Watson, J.B. (1924) *Behaviorism*, Chicago: University of Chicago Press.

Weber, M. (1922/1978) *Economy and Society*, ed. G. Roth and C. Wittich, 2 vols, Berkeley: University of California Press.

White, P.A. (1988) 'Knowing more about what we can tell: "introspective access" and causal report accuracy 10 years later', *British Journal of Psychology* 134: 13–45.

Wilkes, K.V. (1984) 'Pragmatics in science and theory in common sense', *Inquiry* 27: 229–361.

Wittgenstein, L. (1953) *Philosophical Investigations*, Oxford: Basil Blackwell.

—— (1969) *On Certainty*, Oxford: Basil Blackwell.

Wundt, W. (1896) *Lectures on Human and Animal Psychology*, New York: Macmillan.

—— (1920) *Volkerpsychologie.*

Yardley, K.M. (1982) 'On engaging actors in as-if experiments', *Journal for the Theory of Social Behaviour* 12: 291–304.

Zajonc, R.B. (1984) 'On the primacy of affect', *American Psychologist* 39: 117–23.

NAME INDEX

SUBJECT INDEX